Ros Bayley
and
Lynn Broadbent

Published by
Network Educational Press Ltd
PO Box 635
Stafford
ST17 1BF
www.networkpress.co.uk

649.68

© Ros Bayley and Lynn Broadbent 2005
ISBN-13: 978 1 85539 194 9
ISBN-10:   1 85539 194 5

Managing editor: Joanna Chisholm
Design by: Neil Hawkins
Cover by: Neil Hawkins
Cover illustration by: Alisha Hawkins (age 4)
Illustrations by: Leighton Noyes

Printed in Great Britain by Technographic, Colchester, Essex

Contents

Foreword

Everyone worries about literacy. Parents want their children to learn to read and write in order to succeed at school, and the world beyond school. Teachers care about literacy skills because they know such skills are the essential foundation for learning, and governments know a literate population is important for a flourishing economy. Yet, despite everyone's best efforts, many children still have trouble with the 3Rs – reading, writing and arithmetic. Reasons for this are often debated on TV, and newspapers are full of stories about literacy standards and the pros and cons of different teaching methods.

As a literacy specialist for nearly 30 years, I've seen many approaches to teaching come and go (some of them several times), and know there's no 'holy grail' in terms of teaching children to read and write. Certain essential truths, however, are repeatedly proven by research: for example, children who are brought up to love books are more likely to become avid readers than those who aren't; and, in an alphabetic language such as English, phonics is definitely important (see chapter 6 Tuning into sound). But once formal teaching begins, the best teachers remember that all children are different, and what approach works for one child will not necessarily do so for another.

However, there is another essential truth, which research makes clearer every year. Children's experiences **before** they learn to read and write are critically important to their eventual success. **What parents do at home really counts**. This doesn't mean that parents should rush out to buy 'teach your child to read' workbooks and pretend to be teachers. Indeed, this sort of 'early start' philosophy is more likely to do more harm than good – there's a mass of international evidence that pushing young children into formal learning too soon can cause long-term problems, not only educationally but also in terms of emotional development and behaviour.

The sort of parental help that makes all the difference is talking and listening to children, singing with them, reading to them and playfully familiarizing them with language and letter sounds. These activities build strong foundations so that children learn quickly and easily once formal teaching begins.

Flying start with literacy is a magnificent resource in this respect, full of wise advice and great ideas. The activities in this book are carefully structured to lay exactly the right foundations for successful literacy learning, and they also happen to be enormous fun. This is not surprising, as Ros Bayley and Lynn Broadbent are highly respected figures in early years education, and are remarkably knowledgeable about young children and how they learn. Having worked with Ros to create seven-stranded *Foundations of Literacy* (now in use in thousands of schools around the UK), I was thrilled that she and Lynn have written this book for parents, and was honoured to be asked to write the foreword.

I can say with confidence that parents lucky enough to have found this book can stop worrying about literacy. Instead they can settle down to enjoy sharing time and fun activities with their children, while simultaneously aiding their literacy and learning skills.

Sue Palmer
Literacy specialist

Learning to listen

Time to talk

Music, movement and memory

Storytime

Learning about print

Tuning into sound

Moving into writing

Authors' acknowledgements

The authors would like to thank the many parents, carers and early years practitioners who have helped in the compilation of this book. Special thanks go to Sue Palmer for the structure that underpins the publication.

Introduction

Children need good literacy skills. They are the bedrock upon which all other academic learning is based. It is therefore understandable that this is an area where parents really do want the best for their children. The good news is that parents can make a real difference. Recent research clearly indicates that those who actively engage in activities with their children promote both intellectual and social development.

The aim of *Flying start with literacy* is to enable parents and carers to assist children between the ages of three and six in developing the foundations underpinning literacy. There is no mystique in encouraging a child to acquire good literacy skills. In fact, as parents you are probably already doing many of the things that will make a big difference. Using this book will help you to be more aware of what you are doing, so that you can do 'more of what works' as effectively as possible.

Flying start with literacy is divided into seven chapters, with each focusing on an important aspect of development: listening; talking; music, movement and memory; storytelling; print awareness; tuning into sounds; and basic writing. Each chapter outlines the significant skills, knowledge and concepts children need to be successful readers and writers, and give you – the parents – ideas for activities to enhance these. There are also answers to a range of frequently asked questions. Pages 94–95 provide further information on recommended resources and useful websites for those parents who may wish to explore the issues raised at a deeper level.

The important thing about encouraging a child to develop good literacy skills is to relax and have fun. In today's competitive world there are many pressures on parents, but children learn best when they are enjoying themselves. When they feel that they are under pressure, they can 'switch off' and lose interest. It is also important to realize that all children learn differently, and the fact that one child may absorb something more quickly than another does not make them more intelligent. Remember the hare and the tortoise? It may take some children longer than others, but with the right support they can all get there in the end. Lastly, we have sometimes used 'he' and sometimes 'she' throughout the book, but most of what we have to say applies equally to boys and girls or fathers and mothers.

This book will assist you to give your child the necessary support for him to gain a flying start in literacy. We know that you will both really enjoy the process.

Ros Bayley   Lynn Broadbent

chapter **one**

Learning to listen

Listening is perhaps the most important of all the communication skills. If young children cannot listen, they cannot learn, and learning to listen is now harder for children than it has ever been. We live in an increasingly noise-filled world where television, video, DVD and computer games fill our homes with sounds. Life is lived at a faster pace than ever before, and noise is all around us. We simply don't have as much time to listen to each other as we used to. However, with a little positive action you can help your child to become an excellent listener.

In the first instance it is helpful to know a little about the skills involved in listening, as this will help you understand exactly what your child is learning when you play our suggested games. As you play the games he will learn four important skills: discrimination of sounds; social listening; how to develop his aural attention spans; and how to stimulate his auditory memory.

Discrimination of sounds

The ability to detect a foreground sound against background noise is the most basic of all the listening skills. In order to learn language, children must single out their mother's (or their teacher's) voice from the irrelevant background noise of their surroundings. They must also be able to hear your voice in a busy supermarket or pick out their friend's voice in a playground. Once they are able to single out one significant sound, children must learn to distinguish between a widening range of noises: for example, a telephone, a dripping tap or a fire engine. This sort of discrimination needs to come before children can hear similarities and differences in words and the sounds of individual letters.

Playing the following games will really help your child to develop these important skills, which are essential for later work in reading and writing. (See chapter 6 Tuning into sound for further information.)

Statues

You will need: some lively music with a strong beat.
This old party game is an excellent way to teach your child to identify sounds. It can be played quite easily with just one or two family members. In fact, in our experience, young children enjoy this game even when they are the sole player. Tell the players that they can dance to the music but when you shout 'stop' over the top of the music they must freeze like statues. Go on to explain that when you shout 'go' they can begin to dance again. Vary the game by using different kinds of signals: for example, by blowing a whistle or banging on a saucepan.

A listening walk

This is an activity that can happen naturally as part of your daily routine. Any time you are out walking, encourage your child to listen to the wide variety of sounds all around. Get him to spot bird song, dogs barking, neighbours' voices, lawn mowers or the hubbub of the traffic. Play a game where you count how many different noises you can hear. You could also try this activity in a variety of locations.

What sounds can you hear?

Spot the sound

You will need: a collection of items from around the house that make a noise: for example, a squeaky toy, a saucepan lid, a timer or alarm clock, or a bell. Encourage the child or children to listen carefully to each sound. Then play them again but behind a screen and see if the children can identify what has made the sound. A good alternative is to play the game the other way round. Let your child make the sounds for you to guess. When you put them in control, children learn really quickly.

Who is it?

You will need: a dictaphone or a tape recorder on which you or other family members and friends can record a message for your child.
Once you have made a collection of voices, play them to your child and see how many he can identify.

I spy with my little eye

This is an excellent game for developing auditory discrimination. It can be played as soon as your child can hear beginning sounds, that is, the sound that the word begins with as opposed to the name of the letter itself. Say 'I spy with my little eye something beginning with …' (for example, 'd' for 'dog'). Play this game in a variety of locations such as in the garden, kitchen or car.

Answering the telephone

Whenever possible, let your child answer the telephone. Prime other members of the family not to say immediately who they are but to ask your child if he can guess who it is.

Social listening

This type of hearing is used in one-to-one conversation or in small groups. It also involves developing the eye contact that enables the speaker to know that you are attending to their words. Young children learn by being listened to and by looking, watching and copying. Therefore, when you are talking with your child, be sure to make eye contact as she will learn most easily by example. Also, when she is speaking to you, encourage her to give you eye contact. In conversation, urge her to take turns and show your appreciation when she listens patiently and doesn't interrupt. Explain to your child about why it is important to be a good listener and to remember the things that people have told her. When you take time to do this, you help your child to develop skills that will give her a real advantage in an educational situation.

Can you do as I do?

In this simple game, you start by getting your child to focus on your face. Once you have got eye contact, make a series of movements for her to copy: for example, blinking eyes, twitching nose, frowning or smiling. Then switch roles and let your child take the lead in making different facial expressions.

Who has got the toffee?

You will need: a toffee (or other suitable object).
This game can be played with two or more players. Get everyone to put their hands behind their backs and to close their eyes. Once the players have done this, go behind them and place a toffee into one person's hands. The players then open their eyes and take it in turns to guess who has got the toffee, by looking at each other's eyes. It's amazing how guilty you can look if you are the one with the toffee in your hand.

Developing aural attention spans

This involves children in learning to listen and attend for increasingly long periods of time. When children are using a computer game or watching a video, they can play it again or rewind the video if they haven't listened attentively the first time. However, once they are at nursery or school they will not be able to do the same with the teacher's voice, so it is crucial that they develop this important ability. It is also essential that you try not to 'nag' at your children too much. They very quickly develop 'switching off' mechanisms when adults moan too frequently. Listening to stories, poems and songs will help to develop your child's attention span, as will our suggested games.

Spinning bottle

You will need: a plastic bottle.
This game can be played with a few family members. Explain that you are going to spin the bottle and then shout someone's name. The person whose name is called has got to try to pick up the bottle before it stops spinning.

Sausages

You will need: a favourite storybook.
Select a word that appears with reasonable frequency: for example, the name of the main character. Tell your child that you're going to read the story and that he must listen very carefully for your chosen word. Each time he hears it, he is to shout 'sausages'. Once he has got the hang of it, select another word and let the child decide what he will shout when you read the new word.

Music and stories

The suggestions in chapter 3 (Music, movement and memory) and chapter 4 (Storytime) will provide many more opportunities for developing your child's attention span.

Quick responses

You will need: three different 'noise makers' or musical instruments.

The object of this game is for your child to move in a different way in response to each sound that he hears. Talk with your child about how he would like to do this. For example: jump up and down when I bang the saucepan lid; stamp your feet when I blow the whistle; clap your hands when I rattle the beads. Begin by making the sounds quite slowly, then gradually make them faster and faster.

Developing auditory memory

This is a really important skill for learning as it enables children to remember what they have heard, both in the short term and the long term. Playing the suggested games will help your child to develop her short-term auditory memory. Teaching her songs, stories and rhymes by heart will really assist her long-term memory.

The shopping bag

You will need: a shopping bag and a collection of items from the store cupboard.

Place an item in the bag and recite together, 'We went shopping and we bought ...' (for example, a packet of biscuits). Place a second item in the bag and recite again, 'We went shopping and we bought a packet of biscuits and a bottle of squash'. As each additional item is placed in the bag, repeat the list adding the new item. The object of the exercise is to remember the items that have been placed in the shopping bag. Continue until there are too many to be recalled. Play this game at regular intervals and encourage your child to try to beat her own record.

Ted's walk

Make up a short story about Ted (or another of your child's favourite toys). Start off by setting the scene: for example, 'One bright sunny day, Ted decided to go for a walk. He went down the road towards the shops, and the first thing he saw was ...' Take it in turns to choose something that Ted saw and then see how many items you and your child can recall. (Playing this game may even help you to improve your own short-term memory.)

Long, tall Sally

Say the following rap, and each time you recite it add one more person until your child cannot remember any more. 'When long, tall Sally was walking down the alley, Well who do you think she saw? When long, tall Sally was walking down the alley, Well this is who she saw ...'
Get your child to think of ideas for who Sally may have seen, and then repeat the rhyme, adding one more person each time.

Movement directions

Encourage your child to think of all the different ways in which she can move and then choose some of her ideas to give movement directions. Begin by giving one instruction at a time, then two at a time, then three, and so on. For example: jump up and down; spin around; sit cross-legged; touch your toes.

See how many instructions your child can remember.

Do you remember when?

You will need: some old family photographs.
For this activity, encourage your child to recall and talk about the occasions pictured.

My turn, your turn

You will need: a simple screen and two identical sets of 'sound makers' (for example, put some rice into two plastic containers; get two saucepan lids and two spoons to bang them with; put some marbles in two plastic jars; and thread bottle tops on to two pieces of string. You may well also be able to find some whistles or bells around the house). The Early Learning Centre is a good source for inexpensive musical instruments.

Place one full set of sound makers in front of the screen and the other set behind the screen. From behind the screen, play any two of the instruments to your child, placing them down in sequence; remove any instruments that you have not used. Then encourage your child to identify the instruments used and place them in sequence, using her set of sound makers in front of the screen. Finally, remove the screen so that your child can see which instruments she identified correctly. Once your child has got the hang of the game, reverse roles and let her put you through your paces. As your child becomes more used to the game, play three, four or even five sounds in sequence.

On Monday, I ...

This game will also help with learning the days of the week. Get your child to think of something that has happened on each day of the week and then support her when trying to recall the things she has thought of in sequence. This is a good game for playing in the car or at the table during a meal.

Listen for the words

You will need: a favourite story. Explain that you are going to read a story and that every time your child hears a certain word (such as the name of the main character), she is to make a response: for example, touch her nose or scratch her head.

...the big bad wolf...

Hunt the chocolate

You will need: one of your child's favourite chocolates or other sweets. (If you prefer, you can hide a toy instead.)

Hide the chocolate, then tell your child to listen to your instructions, which will lead her to the treat. Encourage her to listen very carefully to your spoken clues as you direct her to where the treat is hidden.

Frequently asked questions

Q : **Why does it sometimes seem as if my child doesn't listen to a word I say?**

A : In the first instance, it is worth keeping a check on the situation over time. Is it that he always seems not to listen, or is it in fact that he is listening selectively? In other words, is he absorbing only the things he wants to hear? If his difficulty with listening is general, then it is certainly worth getting his hearing checked, as temporary hearing loss is very common in young children, especially if they have suffered from ear, nose or throat infections. It may also be worth reflecting on whether you are always sounding as if you are moaning (although you may have plenty to moan about). Young children always respond best to a positive tone, and tend to switch off if you are too negative. In this fast-paced busy world, it is easy to overlook this.

Q : **Why do I seem to have to repeat myself all the time?**

A : As adults we often tend to forget that children see the world very differently to us. The things that seem important to adults may not seem so to them. Therefore, if you have got something really crucial to tell your child, which you really want him to listen to:

● Choose a good time, not one when he is really interested in something else.

● Take time to explain why you need his full attention. Use a phrase something like, 'I really need you to listen very carefully because …'

Q : **I'm worried that my child won't listen to the teacher when she starts school. What can I do to make sure that she does?**

A : Here again, pick a good time, and explain that it is really important to listen as this is the way you learn. (Travelling in the car can be a good time for this sort of discussion, but you will be the best judge of this.) Discuss your worries with your child's teacher, who will be able to suggest ways in which you can help. Most of all, find some time to play some of the games in this chapter, as this will really help to develop your child's listening skills.

Frequently asked questions *continued*

Q : **My child doesn't always seem to hear me when I call her? Do you think she may have a hearing loss?**

A : If you think there may be a problem with her hearing, get your doctor to check it out. Having done this, if there is nothing the matter, it could be that she is either listening selectively or is becoming so engrossed in what she is doing that she genuinely is not hearing you when you call her. Don't automatically assume that she is ignoring you. If she is doing something that she is really enjoying but you need her to listen to you, prepare her for this by giving her a warning. Use a phrase such as, 'I can see that you are really enjoying what you are doing, but in five minutes' time I'm going to need to ask you to put that away as I have something really important that I want to talk to you about ...' This way she has got time to adjust to the idea that she is going to have to change the focus of her attention.

Q : **I have noticed that my daughter's listening skills are much better than my son's. Is there a reason for this?**

A : There are exceptions to every rule, but in general boys have higher activity levels than girls, and this can have an impact on their ability to listen. Boys are all about movement and action and when it comes to sitting still and listening, the odds are stacked against them! Girls can also be energetic and excitable, but when called upon to pay attention, they usually find it easier to calm down and concentrate. Boys can also have growth spurts which can affect their ear canals and lead to significant temporary hearing loss. Hearing difficulties are more common in boys and 70 per cent of boys of school age have poorer hearing than girls! So do be patient, don't ask your son to listen for long periods of time, and when setting tasks or explaining things give clear, precise instructions.

chapter two

Time to talk

In order to learn language you have to use and practise it. Learning to talk is an interactive process, and children won't learn to talk by watching television. Children learn to talk by listening, then imitating what they hear. In fact, they are so good at this that they frequently repeat things that you would rather they didn't. As soon as they are confident with words, they begin to experiment with language for themselves, and once they are doing this their talk becomes really interesting to listen to. By the age of three the 'average' child has a vocabulary of around 1,000 words and can talk in sentences of three, four or more words, linked into long strings by using the word 'and'.

By the age of four, the vocabulary is around 5,000 words, sentences are longer and more complex, and a child will use linking words such as 'cos', 'when' and 'if'.

Because learning to talk is a natural process, it is easy to take it for granted, but you should never underestimate the value of being articulate. Talk is a vital tool for learning, and children who are able to express their thoughts, feelings and needs are at a real advantage. When it comes to getting things down on paper, you have to be able to 'say it before you can write it', so one of the greatest gifts you can give your child is time to talk – and that isn't always easy in a busy world. However, by making time to think about how best to chat with your child, and by trying out some of the suggested activities in this book, you will be really helping to give her the best possible foundations for later work at school.

Supporting and extending talk

Although you may not be aware of it, you are supporting your child's language development every time you play with him. When children are playing, adult talk helps them to absorb new vocabulary and language structures with ease, as there is a direct link between what a child is doing and what you are saying. Most parents do this entirely naturally, but by giving a little time and attention to this process you can become an expert. So next time your child is playing happily:

- Stand back and take a careful look at what is going on.

- Tune into what he is saying and doing and then sit down quietly and begin to play with some of the toys yourself. Unless he talks to you, don't start to talk immediately. (This allows time for you to take in what is happening and allows your child not to be overwhelmed.)

- Once he is comfortable with your presence, engage in some 'self-talk', describing what you are doing with the toys or materials – talking to yourself rather than directly to your child: for example, 'I'm putting all the sheep in this field and all the cows over here.'

- Usually, within a short space of time your child will begin to respond to your self-talk. Once this has happened, you can begin to extend his language as you play alongside him.

Follow your child's lead

When playing with young children, some adults find it difficult to resist the urge to 'take over'. It can require some restraint to follow the child's lead and take turns with him, but it is when you do this that you extend his language most effectively. When deeply engaged in an activity, your child will have a clear sense of purpose, and any attempt to introduce another agenda will only result in frustration and lost opportunities. Use your child's own words as much as you can as this really does give value to what he says. When you repeat your child's words it encourages him to keep talking. Use his comments as conversation openers, for example:

Child: This car go fast … fast … fast … very fast.

Adult: This car goes very, very fast.

Child: That 'cause it racing car.

Adult: That's because it's a racing car. Would you like to drive a racing car?

Expand conversations

This is simply what you would do in any normal conversation, and involves you in introducing new ideas and vocabulary into the discussion.

Use descriptive language

This is just about the most natural way that there is to develop children's language, and there are two ways in which you can do it:

- As your child is playing, simply describe what he is doing as he does it: for example, 'You are putting all of the animals together and there are lots and lots of them.'

- When you play alongside your child, describe your own actions.

As you describe what you or your child is doing, remember to leave some long gaps between sentences so that your child can join in or take over. And if at any time you sense that your child is irritated by your commentary, stop.

Avoid correcting what they say

Young children who are just learning about language structures will make frequent errors as they experiment with language, and how you deal with these errors is really important. If you tell children that they are 'wrong', they can lose their confidence and clam up. Therefore, rather than directly correcting their speech, gently rephrase it using the correct words or phrases. Children learn by listening, watching and copying, and if you model the correct language they will soon get the hang of it.

Avoid asking too many questions

When playing with your child, ask questions sparingly. Questions can put a child on the spot and cause him to freeze up. Show genuine curiosity about your child's play. Show that you are interested and ask him about what he is playing or how he has done something. When you show respect for his ideas, he will offer more and more information about what he is doing.

Vocabulary development

It can take many exposures to a new word before children become confident in using it themselves. The important thing to remember is that you need to link those words to an experience that is already in their lives. That way, you make it easy for them to understand new words. For example, if you wanted to introduce the word 'conflict', the best time to do this would be when you and your child had different ideas about how something should happen, or when she was having an argument with a friend. She then needs time to explore and experiment with new words in order to make them her own. Throughout the early years of life, your child will be learning a wide range of words that are used for different purposes. She will learn words that:

- name: for example, postman, elephant
- denote actions: for example, bring, carry
- describe: for example, friendly, huge, gently
- categorize: for example, jobs, animals (and words that fall in the categories)
- denote position: for example, in, behind, under, between
- denote sequence: for example, when, after
- are used for reasoning: for example, if, but, because, so.

Many of these words will be introduced naturally over time as part and parcel of daily life, but you can help to extend your child's vocabulary by engaging in the following games and activities.

Words that name

You will need: an attractive bag and a collection of interesting objects.
Put the objects into the bag and let your child put her hand into the bag and select an object. Encourage her to see if she can name the object just by feeling it. If she finds this too hard, she can take it out and name it. Introduce one or two unfamiliar objects to provide extra interest. Get her to fill the bag with things for you to name.

Words that denote actions

Perform a simple mime, for example, washing your face, eating a banana or brushing your teeth. Encourage your child to copy the mime and name what you are doing. Swap over, and let your child do an action for you to guess. Another useful game is to write some movement directions on some pieces of card and put them face down on the floor: for example, hop, jump, run, swoop, smile, walk. Pick up a card and let your child perform the action. Swap over and let her pick up cards for you.

Words that describe

You will need: a 'feely' bag of items of different sizes, shapes, textures and colours. Cover your eyes as your child selects an item from the bag. She then hides it and describes it for you to see if you can guess what it is. You may need to show her how to do this by describing an item for her to guess.

Words that categorize

Choose a category (for example, animals, birds, vegetables, vehicles) and together see how many you can name. Keep a record of your previous best, and each time you play the game see if you can beat your record.

Words that denote position

You will need: objects to make an obstacle course in the back garden or somewhere indoors. As your child is enjoying negotiating her way through the obstacle course, label and describe her actions.

Climb on the chair.

Hop on to the stepping stones.

Crawl between the bushes.

Show her how to take a teddy or other favourite soft toy through the obstacles. Encourage her to commentate as she moves around the course: for example, 'over the stones', 'around the birdbath', 'between the bushes' and 'under the chair'.

Words that denote sequence

You will need: several pictures that you took while on holiday or on a day out. Encourage your child to place the pictures in the correct order. As she does so, use words that describe the sequence of events: for example, 'first', 'next', 'later', 'after', 'that' and 'finally'.

Language and thinking

Language is a tool for thinking, and discussion skills form the basis of thinking skills. To become a better thinker, a child must first become better at discussion. When you listen carefully to others, you are thinking; when you weigh your words and stop to reconsider what you and others have said, you are thinking. So, if you want to help your child with thinking skills, the first thing to do is to develop his discussion skills. There are numerous opportunities for doing this as part and parcel of daily life.

When talking with your child in any context, the use of certain types of language will PREPARE (Plan, Recount, Explore, Predict, Analyse, Report and Explain) him for literacy and learning. (Thinking of the word PREPARE helps you to be aware of the different types of language.)

Here are some really simple ways in which you can help your child to develop this essential language. In fact, you will probably realize that you are already doing most of these things. Being aware of what you are doing simply enables you to do it even better.

Plan

This is the type of language that enables you to think ahead and sort things out into sequence (for example, 'first', 'next', 'then'). You can really help your child to develop this type of language when you involve him in planning family events. Encourage him to help plan:

- a family party
- a family holiday
- a shopping trip
- a day out
- his own birthday party
- a picnic.

Recount

This is the type of language that enables you to think back, and involves working out sequence: for example, 'in the beginning', 'after that', 'in the end'. Every time you talk with your child about things that have happened in the past, you will be developing his ability to recount events. So do:

- Encourage your child to tell you about his day.
- Take time to look at family photographs with your child. Ask him: 'Can you remember what happened when …?'
- Take time to answer his questions when he is curious about his family history.
- When you visit relatives, encourage your child to tell them about some of the things he has been doing: for example, 'Tell grandma about when we went to the safari park.'
- Start a souvenir box and collect small souvenirs from visits and outings. Encourage your child to talk about where he got them.
- Once he has a repertoire of stories, ask him to tell you a story.

Explore

This is the type of language that enables you to consider possibilities: for example, 'I wonder what this is?' 'I wonder how this works?' 'Where do you think this should go?' So do:

- Draw his attention to interesting things that you see when out for a walk or a ride in the car.

- When he has a new toy, or you have a new appliance, don't just show him how it works. Instead, take time to speculate and explore.
- Take an interest in the things that fascinate your child … all of those little things he finds under stones and in puddles.

Predict

This is the language you use to anticipate the future, based on what you already know. You can really help your child to develop this type of language by drawing him into discussions that revolve around questions such as:

- What do you think the weather will be like today?
- What do you think will be in this letter/parcel?
- What do you think grandma would like for her birthday?
- What do you think we will see when we get there?
- What do you think you will do at nursery/school today?
- What shall we do when we go on our holidays?
- What do you think will happen to these bulbs we have planted?

Analyse

This is all about expressing thoughts, feelings and curiosity. It's about noticing and observing things, so do take time to:

- Ask your child how he feels about things: for example when he fell over, had a party or did something really well or for the first time.

- Enquire into why things might have happened: for example, when a toy has broken or a friend is not able to come and play.

- Ask him to consider the consequences of his actions: for example, why you are cross/pleased about something he has done.

Report

This type of language enables you to be explicit and describe things in detail. It will involve you in helping your child to be aware of key features such as smell, taste, size, colour and texture. There are a host of everyday situations in which you can help your child develop such language. Simply take the time to:

This banana is yuck!

- Comment on how things taste, smell and feel.

- Urge your child to notice the attributes of things.

- Encourage your child to describe things and events to others: for example, 'Tell grandad about the bird's nest we found in the garden', 'Tell grandma about the dinosaur on the video'.

Explain

This is all about cause and effect, and how and why and curiosity. It can be encouraged by making a few simple enquiries such as:

- Can you tell me about how you did that?

- How did you make that great model?

- Can you explain to grandad how to record his programme on the video?

- Where did you find that beautiful stone?

Having read these easy prompts, you are probably thinking, 'Is it really that simple?' Well actually, yes. In a busy world, the most difficult issue is probably that of finding enough time to listen and talk with your child. When you do make time to do this, you really are giving your child the foundations of literacy. Any time spent listening and talking is time well invested, and remember no one is perfect … you can only do your best.

Frequently asked questions

Q : My problem isn't trying to get my child to talk. It is that my child never seems to shut up. How can I stop her talking as much, especially when I need her to be quiet?

A : Try to see this in a positive way. You know that this isn't always easy when all you want is a bit of peace, but it really is an advantage. Explain to your child that you are really pleased that she has got so much to say, and stress the importance of being a good listener as well. Play some of the games in the previous section to develop her listening skills, and where necessary set aside a special time when you will be available to listen to her. This will help her to manage the times when you need to pay attention to something else.

Q : My daughter seemed to be very forward with talking, but my son doesn't seem anything like as advanced. Why do you think this is?

A : It is now widely accepted that there are distinct differences in the ways that boys and girls acquire and use language. At an early age, girls are more able to articulate words and have more extensive vocabularies than boys. They show more expertise in controlling the dynamics of language. In their speech they pause less, and the quality and length of their sentences is generally more complex. Boys, by contrast, show better abilities in spatial tasks.

Brain scans also show that in females two regions of the brain responsible for processing language are larger than in males. All in all, girls are programmed to process language more effectively, but boys do catch up eventually. It just means that in general you need to be that little bit more patient with boys.

Q : My child refuses to speak at school. What can I do?

A : No one really understands why some children elect not to speak at school. Whatever the reason, you cannot force the issue. Children will converse only when they are ready. Make sure that your child is not being put under too much pressure at school and consult a specialist. This can be arranged either through your GP or through the school.

Frequently asked questions *continued*

Q : **My child still mispronounces a lot of words, especially things with an 's' in.**

A : Firstly, 's' is the most difficult of all the letters to pronounce. Secondly, it takes time for some children to come to terms with the whole range of sounds in our language. Without criticizing or putting pressure on them, simply say words for them slowly and get them to repeat them after you. Try not to show your frustration if they don't pick things up straight away. If the problem continues arrange to get your child's hearing checked. (This is particularly important for boys, who have growth spurts that can affect their ear canals and lead to significant hearing loss.) If there is nothing the matter with your child's hearing and you continue to be worried, arrange for an appointment with a speech therapist. This can be booked through your GP or through your child's nursery/school.

Q : **My child's teacher says that my child is very quiet at nursery/school. I don't know what to do about it as she always has plenty to say at home.**

A : Try hard not to put pressure on your child, as you cannot force her suddenly to become talkative at school. Check out that she is happy and settled. If she is, just be patient. She will talk when she is ready. It is also useful to remember that children will chat about things when they are really interested in something. It may be worth discussing with your child's teacher whether there is anything you can do to help: for example, by letting your child take in something special from home to show and tell the other children about.

Q : **Since starting school my child has 'picked up' some swear words and has started to use them at home, even though we have told her that they are words that we do not wish to hear. How can we stop her from doing this?**

A : Once a child has seen that a word she has repeated has shocked an adult, then that word becomes powerful indeed! She may even repeat it again and again in an attempt to push the boundaries. Whatever you do, stop yourself from over-reacting as this will simply serve to give the word even more power. Stay calm and explain that the word she has used can upset some people, and therefore it is better not to use it. Remember also that you will probably need to point this out several times in order for her to fully understand. With a little concentrated effort the word will then begin to lose its power.

chapter **three**

Music, movement and memory

Most young children love music. It is a natural form of communication that provides a playful context for many different kinds of learning. In fact, the more we learn about how the brain develops, the more we begin to realize just how important music is to a young child. Through music, young children learn many of the skills necessary for later work in literacy. Music develops listening skills, spoken language skills and essential memory skills. As they listen to music, sing songs and learn action rhymes, children learn how to feel and express a beat, and this is really important.

Recent research indicates that a child with good mastery of steady beat is much more likely to do well at school than one who lacks this basic co-ordination. In other words, the ability to maintain a steady beat is a powerful indicator for later academic success, which is hardly surprising when you think about all the things in life that require a steady beat. We need this sense of timing when walking, dancing, writing, cutting with scissors, hammering in a nail, and for much, much more.

A steady beat underlies our ability to pick up the patterns of sound in language. Unless children can do this effectively they cannot learn to read and write language. English is a collection of sounds from lots of different languages, and it is one of the most challenging ones to learn. This makes it even more important that we ground English with a steady beat.

In terms of literacy, one of the key skills is the ability to hear the sounds or 'beats' within words. This is essential for later development in phonics. Music can really help children with this skill. It's also possible that, at a later stage of education, understanding of punctuation and the ability to read with expression have their roots in early rhythm-based activities. So now for the good news – there is a great deal you can do to help your child gain this important skill. In fact, you are probably already doing it, albeit intuitively.

Helping your child to develop a sense of steady beat

A child's first experience of a consistent sound is the thud of his mother's heartbeat while he is in the womb. Then as a baby he is rocked, patted or burped by parents and carers, generally with a regular rhythm. Thus, his sense of steady beat begins to form.

Rhymes and jingles

Make sure your child hears nursery rhymes and songs with a strong beat, such as 'Pat a cake, pat a cake', and encourage him to clap his hands or pat his knees in time to the beat as he listens. To start with when he is young or if he is having difficulty feeling the beat, hold his hands and gently clap them together to the beat. This will really help him to feel the pulse of the music or rhyme.

Make up jingles as you go about your day-to-day activities and chant them together. For example,

We're going up the stairs,
We're going up the stairs,
We're going to have a bath,
We're going to have a bath.

Young children learn by listening, watching and copying. If you make up rhymes and jingles and have fun with language, they will begin to do the same.

When shopping for storybooks, look out for those that are written in rhyme, as these will help with steady beat: for example, *The animal boogie* by Debbie Harter; *Pants* by Giles Andreae and Nick Sharratt; *Brown bear, brown bear, what do you see?* by Bill Martin Jnr and Eric Carle; *Bearobics* by Emily Bolam and Vic Parker; and *No matter what* by Debi Gliori. (This is only a small selection of the many books available.)

Make musical instruments

You will need: plastic containers filled with rice, pasta, pulses or small pebbles.
Play some lively music with a strong beat and shake away to the beat. All children have a natural sense of rhythm and will usually begin to move automatically when they hear some lively music. However, feeling the beat – the strong pulse that underlies the rhythm – may take a little longer to develop. Here again, if your child is experiencing difficulty, gently hold his hands and play together.

You will need: some chopsticks and paper plates. If you have any musicians in the family, get them to provide some music; if not, use a tape or a CD.

Turn the plates over and use as drums. Use the chopsticks as drumsticks. Put on the music and have a steady beat jamming session, drumming away with your child. Involve all the family if they are free. Try using different objects as drums: for example, upturned buckets, saucepans and plastic waste-paper baskets.

Action games

While playing some music with a strong beat on the radio or CD, or providing the beat yourself, encourage your child to do some action games.

While sitting down, pat the beat out using both hands.

While sitting down, pat the beat alternating hands.

While sitting down, stamp the beat using feet alternately.

While standing in one place, walk or march to the beat.

Walk or march to the beat in a forward direction.

Walk or march to the beat in a backwards or sideways direction.

Play 'My turn, your turn'. Point to yourself and say the words, 'My turn', and then perform an action: for example, clap your hands twice to a steady beat. Then point to your child and say, 'Your turn'. Your child then repeats your action. Once he gets the hang of it, he can take the lead.

Simple raps

Rapping allows children to explore the musicality of language. Begin by devising some simple raps and then proceed to more difficult ones. Here are some for you to try out:

Who is knocking at my door?

Ten dirty dogs came knocking at my door,
Rat-a-tat, rat-a-tat, knocking at my door,
Ten dirty dogs came knocking at my door,
Till I said, 'dirty dogs don't do it any more',
So they didn't, but then . . .

(Repeat the rhyme substituting, for example, mucky monkeys, grubby gorillas, cool cats, slithering snakes, and so on.)

Down on the farm

Down on the farm in the middle of the night,
I heard a noise that gave me such a fright,
So I got out of bed to see what I could see,
And there behind the old oak tree . . .
The cows went moo,
The sheep went baa,
The pigs went oink,
The hens went cluck,
The ducks went quack,
The turkeys went gobble,
And the dogs went woof as loudly as they could.

One little caterpillar

One little caterpillar, furry as can be, said,
'I like cabbage for my tea.'
If you like cabbage for your tea
Then clap with me with a one, two, three
One, two, three clap
One, two, three clap
We like cabbage for our tea.

In the bath

I was lying in the bath
When my mum pulled out the plug,
Out went the water,
Glug, glug, glug.
It went gurgle, gurgle, gurgle
As it went down the drain.
Out went my mum
So I filled it up again.

Little raps such as these are easy enough to make up. If you would rather have a book, see the resources list on pages 94–95.

Singing lots of songs

To develop children's articulation in an enjoyable way, encourage them to sing. Songs are also a good method of learning new vocabulary. Sing to your child as you carry out various household chores. You will probably find that, in common with most children today, she learns to sing along with pop songs heard on the television and radio. This is great, but do also try to include in your repertoire:

- nursery rhymes and chants (these are particularly good in terms of preparation for phonics);
- action songs (these develop physical skills important for later work in handwriting);
- songs with choruses for joining in.

First and foremost, have fun. Don't worry if you can't sing like an opera singer or a pop star – your child won't notice. Similarly, don't worry too much about the quality of sound produced by your child, who will still be 'finding her voice'.

Young children have a limited vocal range, so avoid songs that are too high or too low, or she won't be able to join in. If you are unsure about this range, listen out for the tunes she sings to herself while playing. Commercially produced tapes and CDs can also be useful, as they help her maintain the beat – but make sure they are pitched appropriately. (See the resources list on pages 94–95 for useful contacts.)

Which songs?

There are many tapes and CDs of nursery rhymes and songs. Look out particularly for:

- traditional action songs: for example, 'There was a princess long ago', 'In a cottage in a wood', 'Wind the bobbin up', 'Incy wincy spider', 'If you're happy and you know it clap your hands', 'The farmer's in his den';
- traditional songs that can be turned into action rhymes: for example, 'Row, row, row the boat', 'Twinkle, twinkle little star', 'Polly put the kettle on', 'She'll be coming round the mountain when she comes';
- number and cumulative songs: for example, 'Old MacDonald had a farm', 'There were ten in the bed', 'Ten green bottles', 'Five little speckled frogs', 'One man went to mow', 'One, two, three, four, five, once I caught a fish alive'.

Once your child knows a song well, encourage her to be innovative by playing with and changing some of the ideas: for example, old MacDonald could have a shop instead of a farm; or everyone could go round the supermarket instead of the mulberry bush.

Music and memory

As discussed in chapter 1 (Learning to listen), the ability to recall sequences of sound is extremely important for learning, and especially for literacy learning. All musical activities involve remembering sequences of sound, and memorization is made easier by the melody, the rhythm and the repetition. Indeed, if you want to remember something, put it to music – as successful advertising demonstrates. You can use this principle very successfully to help your child learn the alphabet, the days of the week and much, much more.

Action songs and rhymes, marching, chants and raps help children to learn things really easily. Another of their advantages is that they can be repeated again and again without ever becoming boring. Think back to how easily you learned chants and songs in the playground.

The following examples can be used in a variety of ways. Teach your child the rhymes for fun as well as a way of remembering the days of the week, colours, and so on. They can also be used to help with the pronunciation of a range of different sounds.

Quick and slow

This will help with the pronunciation of the long 'oa' sound.

Row, row, row the boat
Slow as slow can be,
Row, row, row the boat
Slowly out to sea.

Row, row, row the boat
Quick as quick can be,
Row, row, row the boat
Quickly out to sea.

Days of the week

This will help with the pronunciation of the long 'ay' sound.

> Monday, a plane to fly far away,
> Tuesday, a scooter to go out to play,
> Wednesday, a ship, we're sailing to Spain,
> Thursday, chuff, chuff, we're off on the train,
> Friday, a rocket to blast into space,
> Saturday, we're in a car in a race,
> Sunday, we sit and we play and we talk,
> Then, when we're ready, we'll go for a walk.

You can devise suitable actions for each vehicle.

Parts of the body

This will help with the pronunciation of the long 'ee' sound.

> Easy peasy, lemon squeezy,
> Stretch your arms and bend your kneezy,
> Easy peasy, lemon squeezy,
> Rub your tum and bend your kneezy.

Encourage your child to think of more actions that can be done to this rhyme.

Colours and directions

This will help with the pronunciation of the long 'igh' sound.

> I'm a kite, a bright red kite,
> I fly to the left, I fly to the right,
> I start off low, I fly up high,
> See me flying in the sky.

This rhyme can be sung to the tune of 'Twinkle, twinkle, little star'.

A counting rhyme

This will help with the pronunciation of the long 'oo' sound.

Oo oo dippity doo, how many tigers in the zoo?
I can count quite a few,
But there's only one kangaroo.
[boo hoo]

Movement and learning

Educators and researchers are fast beginning to realize that movement is essential to learning. Movement awakens and activates the brain, and in children it is actually essential for effective brain development. As children move, the physical effort stimulates powerful brain cell connections. Babies are born with billions of brain cells, yet those brain cells cannot be turned into usable intelligence until they are connected, and movement is essential to this process.

For effective literacy learning, children need to have made good connections between the two hemispheres of the brain. Reading and writing are highly complex tasks, involving the integration of mental activity in both the left and right hemispheres of the brain. For instance, in order to read with understanding, a child must be able to combine:

● phonic decoding (a sequential, analytical processing task associated with the left brain);

● overall comprehension of text (the type of holistic understanding associated with the right brain).

Movement is a key way of helping these connections to form, especially when the physical activity involves controlled and integrated movement on both sides of the body. This may sound complex, but in reality nothing could be easier. You really can help your child make these important brain-cell connections by playing games such as the 'Hokey cokey' and teaching him action songs such as 'The grand old Duke of York'. (For information on more rhymes and CDs, see the resources list, pages 94–95.)

Some action rhymes that will also help with positional language

Point to the left, point to the right.
Thump the air with all your might.
Turn around, slap your thighs,
Run on the spot and lift your legs high.
Arms in the air, reach up high,
Higher and higher till you touch the sky.

Hands at the front,

Hands at the back,

Hands at the front,
Then clap, clap, clap.

Hands up high,

Hands down low,

Then wind the bobbin up,
Let's go, go go.

Put your hands on your hips and sway from side to side,
Now get on your pony and ride, ride, ride.
Hold the reins as you ride down the street,
Then stamp, stamp, stamp, stamp, stamp your feet.

Put one hand on your head, put one hand on your nose,
Now swap them over and touch your toes.
Put one hand at the front, put one hand at the back,
Now swap them over, and clap, clap, clap.
Put one hand on your nose, put one hand on your ear,
Now swap them over, then wipe a tear.

Wobble like a jelly, swim like a fish,
Turn right round, blow a kiss.
Pull on a rope, arms in the air,
Clap your hands, comb your hair.

Move and dance together

In addition to the above activities, you will really be helping your child if you move and dance with him whenever possible. March around the house and garden together. Have some family discos, and do take full advantage of local amenities such as playgrounds and parks. When children are climbing, balancing and crawling, they engage quite naturally in a whole range of movements that will stimulate the brain. If you cannot get to the local park, set up some simple physical challenges in the back garden: for example, use bricks and planks to make objects your child can balance on, or make tunnels for crawling through by taping cardboard boxes together.

Although your child will really enjoy music and movement activities, they are about much more than enjoyment – they will really support your child's learning.

Frequently asked questions

Q : Would it help my child's schoolwork if I paid for music or dancing lessons?

A : If your child shows a special interest in music or dancing, she may benefit from some specialist teaching. However, as far as her schoolwork is concerned, everything she needs can be provided at home. As long as you carry out some of the simple activities in this chapter, and make singing and dancing part of your lives together, your child will not miss out in any way.

Q : I'm not musical in any way, and I certainly can't dance, so how can I help my child?

A : If you are one of those people who will sing only when you're in the car on your own or lying in the bath with the door tightly closed, take heart. Yes, by coming out of the bathroom, you really can assist your child. Everybody can sing and dance. Unfortunately, some of us were led to believe that we couldn't when we were very young. All it takes is an insensitive remark on the part of an adult, and we close our mouths never to sing again. I know adults who will not dance, because at the age of five someone told them that they danced like an elephant.

Fortunately, children won't judge you. They readily accept whatever you do, so do sing and dance with your child. Be sure to be very positive in praising her efforts. In so doing, you really will be supporting her learning.

Q : My child does not seem to be very interested in music or dancing. Will this affect her literacy development?

A : Not necessarily, we are all intelligent in different ways and not everyone likes the same things. The skills that are developed through music and dancing can also be acquired in other ways: for example, through ball games and other outdoor pursuits.

Frequently asked questions *continued*

Q : I've always had a terrible memory. Does this mean that my child will be the same.

A : Not necessarily – remember, her memory can be trained. By engaging in the simple games and activities in this book, you can do much to develop your child's memory skills.

Q : Does it matter what sort of music my child listens to?

A : The best thing for any child is to be able to hear a wide range of different kinds of music. If she is able to do this, she will soon make up her mind about which sorts of music she prefers, so do try to play her some classical music, pop, jazz, world music, and so on. These days, most music can be bought very cheaply. If children are exposed to various types of music, you generally find that they soon start asking for their favourite CDs to be played.

Q : I have heard that listening to classical music, especially Mozart, can boost brainpower. Is there any truth in this theory?

A : As we have pointed out in this chapter, music can help children's literacy learning in a wide variety of ways, but as far as the 'Mozart factor' is concerned, more research is needed. Proponents who specialize in the use of music to accelerate learning suggest that the structured stability of Mozart's music induces a state of 'relaxed alertness' that makes the brain receptive to learning. This may or may not be true, and it may well depend on whether the learner actually likes Mozart! If your child does, then go ahead and play Mozart. You certainly won't be doing any harm.

chapter four

Storytime

S ince time immemorial, stories have been an integral part of growing up. It is
  through stories that most children are introduced to a world where good triumphs
  over evil, and the good guy wins in the end. Stories nourish children's thinking,
extend their vocabulary and help them to learn about the world. Stories are fun, exciting,
sometimes scary, and in terms of literacy learning they play a crucial role. When children
listen to stories, they not only develop important listening skills but also drink in
repetitive, patterned language – the sort of language referred to as 'story language'.

Children brought up on a rich diet of stories are at a distinct advantage when it comes to learning to read and write. They know from experience that stories have a structure, and their ears are trained to the language of stories. When asked to write a story, they can do so with ease, as all of the necessary language has already been internalized through repeated hearings of well-loved tales. Inside their heads they already have all the words with which to describe a setting, develop a plot or bring a character to life – and they don't acquire this sort of language watching television.

Stories on screen are mostly visual: viewers watch the characters and the setting, and they follow the plot with their eyes. Consequently, children who experience stories only through television do not develop a sense of 'joined-up' story. For them, a story is a combination of fragmented dialogue, sound effects and background music. This makes it much more difficult for them to cope with reading and writing for themselves – those patterns are simply not there.

However, if you are a parent or carer wanting to give your child the best possible start to his literacy learning, you can immerse him in story language simply by reading aloud to him and telling stories on a daily basis. In so doing, you will be giving him a massive boost.

Storytelling and listening skills

Storytelling develops all aspects of listening. When you tell a story, rather than read one, you are free to make eye contact with your child and can use facial and vocal expression, gesture and body language to maintain his interest. The rhythmic, repetitive, patterned language of stories such as 'The gingerbread man' will develop his attention span and auditory memory. With repeated telling, it won't be long before your child is joining in with relish.

If you feel a little nervous about launching into a story without a book, try reading the story into a tape recorder, then play it back a few times, joining in as you begin to commit it to memory. And remember, anyone can tell a story. You don't need any special qualifications, and it doesn't matter if you make a mistake. In fact your child will love it when you get it wrong and will positively enjoy putting you right. Start with something you feel confident with and gradually build up your repertoire.

Some traditional stories for telling

The following stories have well-developed characters, lots of repetition, a build-up of plot and a happy ending:

- 'The gingerbread man'
- 'Goldilocks and the three bears'
- 'Little red riding hood'
- 'Three billy goats gruff'
- 'Jack and the beanstalk'
- 'The little red hen'
- 'The three little pigs'
- 'The enormous turnip'
- 'Chicken licken'.

Storytelling using toys and props

In common with most young children, your child will probably have at least one much-loved soft toy, so why not make use of this favourite character as a focal point for storytelling? There are a variety of ways in which you can do this:

- Take the toy out with you on walks and family outings, and photograph it in a wide variety of settings. You can then use these photographs as a basis for making a book and storytelling. Stick the photographs into a scrapbook and let your child tell the story of what happened: for example, Ted's trip to the dentist or the hairdresser; Ted's visit to the park or the library.

- Plan something special for the toy and make a photographic record: for example, a party or a trip to the cinema.

- Make up some stories about the toy's adventures: for example,
  - the day Ted got lost
  - Ted's new clothes
  - Ted gets left in the garden/locked in the car all night
  - Ted sneaks out to the park at night
  - Ted is frightened
  - Ted hides and no one can find him.

Some other ideas for supporting storytelling are:

- Invest in some inexpensive finger puppets or glove puppets and use them as a basis for storytelling. (See the resources list on page 94.) If you can find the time, make your own puppets from wooden spoons, paper plates, paper bags or old socks.

- Get out your old family photograph albums showing your soft toys from when you were a child, and tell stories about your own childhood.

- Collect some interesting props (for example, a small treasure box, some interesting old coins, a 'magic' whistle or an old key) and use them as a basis for your own stories. By posing a few simple questions, a story will begin to unfold. For example, if you had an interesting old key you might ask:

> I wonder who might have a key like this?

- What door might this key open?

- Who does the key belong to?

- Is it perhaps the key to a box, and what might the box contain?

- Is the key a magic one?

Your child will really enjoy it when you make up stories for her. They do not need to be complicated – you don't have to be Hans Christian Andersen. Your stories will have infinite appeal to your child simply because they are your stories. Keep the plot simple and be sure to include lots of repetition, because this will make your story memorable and enable your child to retell it for herself. Your character could go for a walk and find/do numerous things, for example, or she could meet various people; or there could be a series of ways of solving a problem ('first' … 'next' … 'in the end').

Once you get into storytelling, you soon realize that all stories seem to fit into a set of universal themes, such as:

- getting lost or losing something
- finding something interesting
- helping someone
- feeling afraid
- split loyalties
- disappointment
- making choices/moral conflict
- breaking rules
- acting bravely
- being surprised
- endeavour
- getting into trouble
- feeling jealous
- being bullied/picked on
- winning and losing
- mistaken identity
- accidents
- not thinking ahead
- dishonesty
- taking revenge
- getting locked in/trapped
- journeys and quests.

Telling stories by heart

When you and your child tell stories by heart you will not only be developing your child's auditory memory (something that is important for all aspects of learning) but you will also be familiarizing her with key sentence constructions. This will really assist her in later work in writing. Once a story is familiar, sit back and let your child take over. If she loses the thread, you can provide a prompt (the next phrase or action), until eventually she is telling the whole story for herself.

Role playing with your child

To make your storytelling even more enjoyable, role-play the stories with your child, using props, or let her act them out on her own. You'd be amazed at the number of simple, everyday objects that can be used: for example,

- for 'The three bears', set the table with three bowls and spoons in various sizes and provide some porridge;
- for 'Jack and the beanstalk', provide a packet of seeds, a large pair of Wellington boots and paint a hard-boiled egg with gold paint;
- for 'The three billy goats gruff', make a simple bridge in the back garden.

Having set up the props, you and your child can act out the appropriate story, or she can role-play the scene for you.

Build up a collection of stories on tape and CD

Stories on tape and CD are available to your child all the time. In today's busy world, you cannot be constantly available to read stories at the drop of a hat; but if your child has a good selection of stories on tape or CDs which you or a member of your family has compiled she will be able to hear her favourite stories whenever she wants.

Make stories while you play

You will probably have noticed that, when your child is playing with her favourite toys, she quite naturally makes up stories as she plays. Take time to listen to her stories. Ask questions about these tales and help your child to expand her ideas. Play with the toys yourself and build up stories of your own … this will really help your child to extend her own thinking.

As you tell stories with your child you will be increasing her vocabulary, sentence structure and confidence. She will soon be eager to tell the stories for herself. And that's not all – listening to lots of stories and making up her own means that, when she eventually comes to write stories, she won't struggle to invent characters, settings and plots … she will have all of these at her fingertips.

Reading stories aloud

Some children are lucky enough to learn to read 'naturally' as their parent or carer sits alongside them and reads favourite books again and again. Gradually, the child begins to join in until he can 'read along'. Initially he is simply reciting what he has learned by heart, but as a result of this sort of enjoyable activity, the child gradually begins to recognize certain words and to associate letters with sounds.

One little pig built a house of straw.

The more you share books with your child, the more likely he is to become one of these 'natural' readers. Through daily story sessions he will be learning:

- how to hold a book the right way up
- that books have a front and a back
- how to turn the pages correctly
- how to tell a story through the pictures

- that text conveys meaning
- that text goes from left to right and top to bottom (when reading English).

He will gradually begin to notice and identify:

- letters that are in his name
- letters that are the same.

After lots and lots of experience, he will begin to:

- point to words
- recognize certain words

- try to make the words fit the text.

So do:

- make some time each day to share stories with your child
- build up a collection of quality picture books to share with your child.

Below is a list of 'classic' picture books. These are tried-and-tested favourites and well worth adding to your collection:

- *Alfie gets in first* by Shirley Hughes (Red Fox)
- *Amazing Grace* by Mary Hoffman (Frances Lincoln)
- *Angry Arthur* by Hiawyn Oram and Satoshi Kitamura (Red Fox)
- *Billy's sunflower* by Nicola Moon (Little Hippo)
- *Brown bear, brown bear, what do you see?* by Bill Martin Jnr and Eric Carle (Puffin)
- *Danny's duck* by June Crebbin (Walker)
- *Dear daddy* by Philippe Dupasquier (Puffin)
- *Dear zoo* by Rod Campbell (Puffin)
- *Dr. Dog* by Babette Cole (Red Fox)
- *Dogger* by Shirley Hughes (Picture Lions)
- *Duck in the truck* by Jez Alborough (Collins)
- *Each peach pear plum* by Janet and Allan Ahlberg (Puffin)
- *Elmer* by David McKee (Red Fox)
- *Farmer duck* by Martin Waddell (Walker)
- *Funnybones* by Janet and Allan Ahlberg (Puffin)
- *Gorilla* by Anthony Browne (Red Fox)
- *Hairy Maclary from Donaldson's dairy* by Lynley Dodd (Puffin)
- *Handa's surprise* by Eileen Browne (Walker)

- *Hector's new trainers* by Amanda Vesey (Picture Lions)
- *It was Jake!* by Anita Jeram (Walker)
- *Jamaica and Brianna* by Juanita Havill (Heinemann)
- *Little rabbit Foo Foo* by Michael Rosen and Arthur Robins (Walker)
- *Mister Magnolia* by Quentin Blake (Red Fox)
- *Mr Gumpy's outing* by John Burningham (Red Fox)
- *My cat likes to hide in boxes* by Eve Sutton and Lynley Dodd (Puffin)
- *Not now, Bernard* by David McKee (Red Fox)
- *One snowy night* by Nick Butterworth (Collins)
- *Owl babies* by Martin Waddell (Walker)
- *Pass it, Polly* by Sarah Garland (Puffin)
- *Pass the jam, Jim* by Kaye Umansky and Margaret Chamberlain (Red Fox)
- *Peace at last* by Jill Murphy (Macmillan)
- *Rosie's walk* by Pat Hutchins (Red Fox)
- *So much* by Trish Cooke (Walker)
- *Solo* by Paul Geraghty (Hutchinson)
- *Suddenly!* by Colin McNaughton (Picture Lions)
- *Tall inside* by Jean Richardson (Puffin)
- *The bear under the stairs* by Helen Cooper (Red Fox)
- *The elephant and the bad baby* by Elfrida Vipont and Raymond Briggs (Puffin)
- *The gingerbread boy* by Ian Beck (Oxford University Press)
- *The tiger who came to tea* by Judith Kerr (Collins)
- *The time it took Tom* by Nick Sharratt (Scholastic)
- *The train ride* by June Crebbin (Walker)
- *The very hungry caterpillar* by Eric Carle (Puffin)
- *This is the bear* by Sarah Hayes and Helen Craig (Walker)
- *Through my window* by Tony Bradman and Eileen Browne (Mammoth)
- *Tortoise's dream* by Joanna Troughton (Puffin)
- *We're going on a bear hunt* by Michael Rosen and Helen Oxenbury (Walker)
- *Where the wild things are* by Maurice Sendak (Red Fox)
- *Where's my teddy?* by Jez Alborough (Walker)
- *Where's Spot?* by Eric Hill (Puffin)

Frequently asked questions

Q : **My child seems to prefer to watch television rather than listen to a story. Will this affect her literacy development?**

A : It is quite possible that it could. Your child will be absorbing different types of language when watching television. Only by sharing books will her ears become attuned to the language needed for reading. However, it is not a good idea to force her to sit and listen to a story when she doesn't want to, as this could actually make her even more resistant to books and stories. Instead, tune into what she is most interested in and try to find really attractive books that match her inclinations. Take her into a bookshop or the local library and let her choose some books for herself.

Boys in particular often prefer information books to stories, and sharing an information book with your child is just as valuable as reading a story. As long as you have some really colourful and exciting books around, you will probably find that he will pick them up in his own good time. And in the unlikely event that he doesn't, try involving him in taking photographs that can be made into books in which he is the star.

Q : **My child likes to read the story for herself, but she's only doing it from memory. She's not really 'reading'. Is this alright?**

A : Absolutely; memorizing a story is a vital part of learning to read. As she does this, gently draw her attention to the words, saying something like, 'Look. You have just read all the words on that page.' (Do this even if she has not read them completely accurately.) You will really be boosting her confidence, and before long she will be linking what she has remembered to the actual words. It's as if memorizing the story acts as a bridge to the words themselves.

Q : **What sort of books can I buy to best help my child learn to read?**

A : Look for books with good stories and great illustrations. (Our recommended list on pages 51–52 should help you here.) But most of all choose books that match your child's interests. If you are in doubt, don't be afraid to pop into nursery or school and ask your child's teacher to make some recommendations.

Frequently asked questions *continued*

Q: My child asks for the same story again and again and again, to the point where I know it off by heart. Is this normal?

A: Yes, indeed, it is quite normal for a child to develop a firm favourite from the range of stories you read to her. She loves the book so much that she wants to return to it again and again. If you ask her why she likes the book so much, she may be able to explain her reasons. However, if she can't express why, you can take it that there will be some aspect of the story that she needs to explore over and over again until she has made sense of it. Once she has done this, much to your relief, she may then stop asking for that particular story. Don't be lulled into a false sense of security, the next favourite will soon emerge.

Q: Some fairy stories and traditional tales seem to be very frightening. Will this be harmful to my child?

A: Read in the right way, these stories should be helpful rather than detrimental. For children who are lucky enough to be cared for in ways that enable them to feel happy and secure, fairy stories are an excellent way of introducing them to the idea that not everything about the world is 'nice'. In the safety of their home and with people they love, they can explore these ideas in the knowledge that it is only a story, and anyway, unlike real life, good always triumphs over evil in the end. Besides which, who doesn't enjoy being frightened just a little bit?

Q: My child seems much more interested in comics than in books. Is this a bad thing?

A: Children benefit from exposure to lots of different kinds of literature, and comics can be a great starting point. In fact, children can learn a lot about reading from spending time with comics. All of the points on page 50 can be applied to comics. Follow your son's interest to see what he finds most interesting in his comics. Once you have done this you will be able to find books with similar characters and themes.

chapter five

Learning about print

As long as children have plenty of opportunities for conversation, then learning to talk is an entirely natural process. Learning to read and write, however, is not. As we pointed out in chapter 4 (Storytime), some lucky children learn to read apparently effortlessly through sharing plenty of books with adults, but we cannot assume this will just happen. Many children need a great deal of support in order to unravel the complexities of print. Their learning can be made much, much easier when they are supported by adults who know how to help them. In this chapter we help you to become aware of the range of ways in which you can support your child as he treads the path towards becoming a confident reader.

To many young children, print is invisible – it is so meaningless to them that they don't even notice it. To others, it is merely one sort of mysterious squiggle among many – like patterns on wallpaper. Children have to learn that print is significant. They have to recognize that writing is different from pictures, and that words and letters are different from numbers. In fact, as soon as your child starts noticing print, it is really important that you use this terminology with him.

Children also have to know what reading and writing are for, and how people do it: for example, in English, print goes from left to right and top to bottom of the page. Finally, they must be familiar with the letters of the alphabet, and how these are used to make up words. Helping your child to understand the nature and function of print is an important element in laying the foundations of literacy. What's more, it's not at all difficult to do.

Awareness of print

Next time you're out and about, spend just a few moments noticing how much print you can see. If you take the trouble to look, it soon becomes evident that print isn't something that's confined to books – it's actually everywhere, but you don't necessarily notice it until someone draws your attention to it. One of the most powerful things you can do to help your child become aware of print is to draw his attention to it. This can be very useful if the print has meaning for your child. Consider for a moment the impact of words and phrases such as 'toy shop', 'playground', 'this way to the rides' and 'pets corner'. They hold infinite interest for a child, and by pointing out such signs you really can help him to understand the nature and function of print.

Noticing printed matter at home

Once you start consciously to look out for printed material, you will see it in unexpected places, such as at the breakfast table: cereal packets are a wonderful source of print, for example. You can also check out the text on sweet wrappers, clothes and toiletries. Curiosity is the name of the game, and the more you have fun noticing print, the more your child will do the same.

Looking out for signs

When you're out shopping, in the car, on the top deck of the bus or on holiday, see how many signs you can find. Read words aloud such as 'stop', 'exit', 'fire exit', 'toilets', 'open', 'closed' and 'menu'. Discuss each sign and why it's there. Ensure that your child knows exactly what it means. Some signs and notices appear in many different places, and once your child is familiar with them he will really enjoy spotting them. Variations on the word 'out', for example, appear in a variety of locations: 'check out', 'keep out', 'way out', 'out of order', and so on.

Letter spotting

You can also enjoy picking out letters and speculating on what they stand for: for example, 'P' for parking, 'L' for learner, 'I' for information, 'S' and 'P' for salt and pepper, 'B and B' for bed and breakfast, 'H' and 'C' on hot and cold taps, 'M' for McDonald's.

Alphabet knowledge

An important part of awareness of print is recognizing and being able to name the letters of the alphabet, so it is helpful if you can teach your child to recite the letters of the alphabet as soon as she is able. A really easy way to do this is to teach her an alphabet song and link it to an alphabet book or an alphabet chart or wall frieze. Sing the song yourself, pointing to the letters as you sing. Your child will soon be joining in. Refer to the letters by their alphabet names (ay, bee, cee). At this stage, alphabet knowledge has nothing to do with phonics, so this is not a case of 'k' for 'cat'.

Alphabet song

A really easy alphabet song is the 'Alphabet tea song', which is sung to the tune of 'Bobby Shaftoe'. It goes like this:

    a b c d e f g

    all the letters came to tea,

    h i j k l m n

    the food was quite delicious,

    o p q r s t u

    v and w they came too,

    x and y ate all the pie,

    and z washed up the dishes.

Make your own alphabet book

You will need: a scrapbook, some old calendars, magazines and catalogues, and some family photographs.
Label each page of your scrapbook with the letters of the alphabet. Then start to create a collection of pictures that begin with the various letters. See how many pictures you can collect for each letter. Include photographs of family members and places you and your child have visited, because these will have a special meaning and be more easily recalled. To make the game even more enjoyable, focus on items that are interesting to your child – the toy section of a catalogue is always very useful for this purpose.

Using letters

A child who is familiar with the alphabet will know what letters are, and also that there are a limited number of them. (Without this knowledge, learning to read could be an impossibly daunting task.) You will probably find the letters that most interest your child will be those in her name, so do take advantage of this to help develop her knowledge. When it is her birthday, for example, encourage her to place the letters of her name on her birthday cake. She is also likely to enjoy forming her name with magnetic letters on the fridge door.

Your child may even be keen to write her name. If she is, help her to do so, but don't pressurize her in case her eyes and finger muscles are not fully mature (see chapter 7 – Moving into writing). Let her play with letters, as the more she does this before reading and writing begins in earnest the more confident she'll be when it comes to tackling phonics and writing. The following are some other ways in which you can help your child to learn about the alphabet.

Alphabet treasure hunt

You will need: wooden, plastic or magnetic letters. (If you don't have these, write the letters on to pieces of card.)
Hide individual letters in the house and the garden: for example, the specific letters in your child's name. Ask her to hunt for them.

Alphabet washing line

You will need: an alphabet frieze, a length of string and some pegs. Inexpensive alphabet friezes and posters are readily available in a wide range of shops nowadays. Alternatively, if you already have a frieze or poster and your child is familiar with the letters of the alphabet, you could cut this up so that you can play games with the letters.

Secure each end of the string to make a washing line at a suitable height for your child. Then ask her to peg the letters on the line in sequence. Once she is able to do this, she could pick out the letters of her name, or form the names of other family members or friends.

What's missing?

You will need: pieces of card and a pair of scissors.

If your child is at the stage where she can recognize some words (for example, her name and words such as 'mum', 'dad' and 'love from'), write out the words on pieces of card, leaving space for one or more of the letters. Then write the omitted letters on separate pieces of card. See if your child can identify the missing letter or letters and place them in the spaces. You can even conceal the letters and tell her that they have been stolen by the alphabet thief. See if she can find the missing letters – children always enjoy a hunt.

When you are cooking

Children love to help with the cooking. Whenever you are making pastry or biscuits, help your child to mould leftover dough to make the letters of her name or the names of other family members. (You can also buy moulds in the shape of letters for this purpose.) If, like many parents and carers, you find you don't have too much time for cooking, shop around for biscuits and other food items in the shape of letters. Once you start to look you'll be amazed at how many things you can find. While you enjoy eating the food shapes, you can also have some very useful conversations about the alphabet.

The significance of print

Chapter 4 (Storytime) described how much children learn about print when you share storybooks with them on a regular basis. However, as well as fiction, children need to learn about other forms of print that are important in daily life: for example, recipes, posters, letters, the phone book and information books. They need to know what they are for and how they are organized. You can really help here by explaining what you are doing, and why, each time you use a recipe, an instruction manual or a directory. Try to take advantage of every opportunity to show how and why adults read.

Demonstration is also the best way to teach your child about writing. Each time you write anything, give your child a running commentary on what you are doing, and why, and take time to answer his questions. He will soon learn about the importance of writing.

Take time to talk to him about:

- your shopping list (invite him to help you compile the list and let him see you write down his suggestions)

- notes to the milkman

- 'to do' lists

- emails you send

- letters and cards you send to friends and family members

- your diary and family calendars

- labels you write

- the books and magazines that are important to you. Tell him about why they are important to you and how they give you pleasure.

As he becomes aware of the importance of print, he will want to 'help' you with your writing. He will begin to scribble for himself in an attempt to copy what he has watched you doing. Once he starts to do this, it is extremely important not to criticize him, even if he is not writing correctly. The 'writing' he is doing is absolutely right for his stage of development. Even if it looks like 'scribble' to you, do compliment and praise his efforts. This way he will take even more interest in writing and be even more enthusiastic about trying to write for himself. Remember, the more he gets the opportunity to watch adults writing, the more he will learn about the process, especially when you take time to describe what you are doing. Children learn best from the people they love and respect, and because you are very important to them they will want to know about, understand and copy the things that you do.

Take time to observe your child as he interacts with text in all its forms. Notice what he is aware of and what he doesn't yet understand. By doing this you will gain a far better idea of how to help him move on to the next level of understanding. Most of all, be patient. Learning about print is a long-term process. Children's knowledge extends little by little as they build on their experience of the world.

With the right support, all children will build this understanding. It is utterly unimportant that some will do this more quickly than others. What matters is that you maintain your child's interest, enthusiasm and curiosity. You can then be sure that in his own good time he will learn everything he needs to know about print.

Send some communications through the post

All children love it when it is their birthday, and receiving birthday cards is an excellent way of learning about print. Why not post cards to your child at other times of the year? You can send cards that feature special characters or interests. You might even consider sending messages to your child's favourite soft toys.

Treasure hunt

You will need: a small gift for your child, pieces of paper and something to write with. Explain that you have a special gift for your child, which you have concealed. In order to find it, he must follow a series of clues. Write and hide the clues. Then help him to follow the clues as he searches for the treasure.

Leaflets and lists

When you are out and about, pick up leaflets: for example, from the health centre, shops, take-away food restaurants and garden centres. Read them and tell your child what they say.

When you are playing with him, take advantage of naturally occurring opportunities to add writing to the play: for example, if you are pretending to be hairdressers, make an appointment book; if you are playing schools, make a register; and if you are being garage mechanics, have a jobs list.

A family diary

You will need: a large desk diary and something to write with.

Use the diary to record events that have been significant for you and your child. If possible, add photographs and invite your child to invent captions for them. He will really gain in confidence as he sees you writing down his words. Similarly, you could compile a diary of adventures for a favourite soft toy.

A family message board

You will need: a large message board and a board marking pen.

Divide up the board so that each member of the family has a section. When someone needs to remember something (for example, a doctor's appointment), let your child see you write this on the board. By doing this, you are directly demonstrating how you use print to organize your life. The message board can be used to communicate 'fun' messages, too: for example, 'Daddy, please don't eat the cream cakes that are in the fridge'. Use it also to remind yourself and your child of television programmes that you both don't want to miss.

Frequently asked questions

Q : **I found it difficult to learn to read. Will my child have the same problems?**

A : Not necessarily. There doesn't appear to be any exact pattern. Some children learn easily, even though their parents didn't, and the reverse is also true. No one is as yet entirely sure why this is the case. Everyone's brain is 'wired' differently, and some children are lucky enough to be 'wired' in such a way that reading comes easily to them.

The important point is that learning to read is not a race. With the right support, all children get there in the end. So try not to show too much anxiety if your child does seem to be taking longer than her friends. Continue to do all the things suggested in this chapter and do share your anxieties with your child's teacher. If your child senses that you are concerned, she will lose confidence and see herself as a failure. If she seems anxious, assure her that she will soon be reading if she perseveres. With your support and confidence behind her, she cannot fail. It is when children believe that they are unsuccessful that they lose heart and give up.

It is also worth remembering that, in the British education system, children are asked to start reading at an alarmingly early age. If they lived in other parts of the world they wouldn't even be starting school until they were six and in some cases nearly seven.

Q : **Most writing is done on the computer these days, so my child doesn't seem to see us 'writing' very often. Will this affect her development?**

A : It's important that children have access to a wide range of different communications, so try to write with your child some of the time, explaining what you are writing and why. Do the same thing when you are sending a communication by email or text. Point out and comment on writing when you see other people doing it: for example, in shops and restaurants. The more you talk with your child about print in all its forms, the more she will come to understand what print is and why adults use it.

Frequently asked questions *continued*

Q : **My child doesn't seem interested in print. What can I do about this?**

A : Keep doing all of the things suggested in this chapter. Most of all, help your child to experience print in ways that are really meaningful to her: for example, send her a parcel through the post, which is explicitly addressed to her. Put something inside that you know she will really like, and include a special message. Suggest that there may be further communications. This will grab her attention and mean that she will be waiting for the postman. When something relates to her personally, your child will usually be fascinated by it. Remember also that it is quite natural for some children to become attracted to print before others. Everyone has different interests. However, with the right support, children learn about print in their own good time.

Q : **My daughter and her friend are in the same class, but her friend seems so much more advanced. She is already reading simple books. My daughter can't read at all yet. Does this mean that she is not as intelligent?**

A : Not at all. The age at which a child starts to read is not necessarily an indication of intelligence. The ability to read depends upon a wide range of factors, some of which are physical and have little to do with intelligence: for example, the eye muscles need to have developed sufficient strength to enable a child to focus, track and concentrate on reading. For some children, this happens much sooner than for others. As experienced teachers of young children, we can tell you without hesitation that children who begin reading at a very early age are frequently overtaken by those who start much later. Some children demonstrate readiness for reading at a very early age, whereas others may not 'take off and fly' until they are approaching seven, and for some children even later. The most important thing you can do is to encourage rather than 'push' your child, reassure her that it isn't a race and let her know you have every confidence in her abilities.

NB If you suspect that your child may have sight difficulties, arrange for her to see an optician. If such difficulties go undetected, they could make learning to read considerably more difficult.

chapter six

Tuning into sound

Detecting word and letter sounds in the English language is a crucial part of learning to read and write. Much of this tuning in occurs as children listen to and memorize songs and nursery rhymes (see chapter 3 – Music, movement and memory). In fact, it is becoming increasingly clear that children with good rhyming skills often become good readers. The repetitive, patterned language of nursery rhymes is ideal for encouraging a young child's ears to become accustomed to the sounds of speech. But there is a problem. In today's hectic world, children are not learning nursery rhymes in the way that they used to, and unfortunately this is having a very detrimental effect on their literacy development.

In gaining early literacy skills, children pass through two main developmental stages: phonological awareness (an awareness of the sounds in language) and phonemic awareness (the realization that a word can be taken apart and put together again, for example, d/o/g = dog). Reciting nursery rhymes and songs helps a young child to become phonologically aware, which is very important for later work in phonics. But before a child can go on to develop phonemic awareness, he must pass through a number of other developmental stages. Once you have an understanding of these, you are well placed to know where your child is in his development. This in turn will enable you to support him in his learning.

Phonological awareness

This term means awareness of sounds in language. A child must be able to distinguish different sounds in language before he can go on to develop phonemic awareness – the ability to hear individual speech sounds. The stages of phonological awareness are:

● Awareness of words as units of sound. As long as children have opportunities for lots of conversation, this will happen naturally within the first two years of life.

- Awareness of syllables, that is the recognition that words are made up of more than one sound. Again, for children who engage in plenty of talk and sing songs with adults, this should happen naturally.

- Awareness of rhyme. The average three year old is usually conscious of rhyme. He will enjoy joining in with and learning to recite simple rhymes, and once he is aware of rhyme he will take great delight in making up his own: for example, 'It's easy, weasy, peasy, deasy'. The words he invents may not be proper words, but by the way he plays with language he is telling you that he understands rhyme. Once a child is doing this, he is well on the way to the next stage, as he is gradually alerted to initial sounds (in the example above, 'w', 'p', 'd'). From this, you can probably appreciate why songs and rhymes are extremely important in child development.

So tune in and listen carefully to the way your child uses and plays with words, as this will help you to understand where he is in the development of these 'awarenesses'.

To support the development of phonological awareness, take time to do the following activities with your child.

Reading nursery rhyme books

Build up a collection of nursery rhyme books and stories that are written in rhyme. After a few readings you will find that your child will take pleasure in joining in. When he knows a book well, you can stop at certain points in the reading and let him 'fill in' the rhyming word. Some particularly good books are:

- *Pass the jam, Jim* by Kaye Umansky and Margaret Chamberlain (Red Fox)

- *Pants* by Giles Andreae and Nick Sharratt (Oxford University Press)

- *Where's my teddy?* by Jez Alborough (Walker)

- *The animal boogie* by Debbie Harter (Barefoot)

- *The grumpalump* by Sarah Hayes (Walker)

- *Doing the animal bop* by Jan Ormerod and Lindsey Gardiner (Oxford University Press)

- *The park in the dark* by Martin Waddell (Walker)

- *Bumpus jumpus dinosaurumpus!* by Tony Mitton and Guy Parker-Rees (Orchard)

Make up rhymes

As you go about your daily activities, think up rhymes. They can be quite simple, so there's no need to feel daunted by the idea. Examples of simple rhymes are:

We've got to go to school,
We know it is a rule.
We like it anyway,
As with our friends we play.

We're going in the bath,
We're going to have a laugh.
Don't be such a dope,
You're sitting on the soap.

I don't like coffee and I don't like tea,
But I do like sitting on grandad's knee.

Where is the rhyme?

Once your child has had lots of exposure to rhyme, you can build on this experience by playing rhyming games. Take it in turns to think of words that will rhyme with a simple word such as 'cat': for example, 'mat', 'hat', 'fat', 'bat', 'sat', 'rat', 'pat'. Try not to worry too much if your child comes up with words that are not 'proper words'. The important thing is that she is hearing the rhyme. You can also collect pictures and objects of things that rhyme: for example, a sock, a rock, a clock and a lock; a man, a can, a van, a pan and a fan.

Phonemic awareness

Once your child is aware of rhyme, she will be well on her way to developing phonemic awareness, which is the realization that a word can be taken apart and put together again, as in d/o/g/ = dog. At these early stages, children still need to hear lots of rhymes and tongue twisters, as this will help them to develop clear articulation. Gradually, however, you can begin to 'sound out' words orally for your child. You can do this by playing little guessing games such as 'I am thinking of a p/i/g/'. Instead of saying the whole word, split it up into individual syllables and see if your child can guess what you are thinking of. Once she gets the hang of it, she can have a go at splitting up words for you to guess.

At this point this game should be entirely oral, and the sounds should not be written down. This is all about helping your child to hear the individual sounds within words, so that when the time comes she can make the link between the sound she is hearing and the written symbol she is seeing. Before she will be able to do this, however, she must be able to hear the sound. The following activities will help your child develop phonemic awareness.

Splitting word games

When out for a walk, why not try splitting up movement words into syllables? For example: shall we h/o/p/, r/u/n/ or s/k/i/p/?

Themed scrapbook

Why not collect pictures of things beginning with different sounds?

Make up some jingles

Do this by focusing on different sounds, for example:

- Jamie ate a juicy jelly.
- Cool and clever cat can climb.
- Dirty Dan dived for a dare.
- Betty had a big balloon.

Letter sounds

When in the house, out on a walk or travelling in the car, why not choose a letter sound and see how many things your child can spot beginning with that sound?

Play I spy

Place some three-letter objects on a tray: for example, a cup, a tin, a hat, a bag and a pot. Then say, 'I spy with my little eye a t/i/n/' and invite your child to pick up the object. Once she gets the hang of it, you can swap over.

Phonics: associating the sound with the letter

Once your child can hear, say and remember a range of sounds she is ready to begin to link these sounds with specific letters or groups of letters. (If your child experiences difficulty in doing this, don't try to force things as it means that she needs more time to hear the sounds, so go back to the activities that will help her develop phonemic awareness. Any attempt to force the issue will only confuse her and undermine her confidence.)

Very often, a child will tell you she is ready to make this link, by pointing to letters and saying something like, 'Look, that's a "b" like in my name.' You will probably find that she spots similarities and differences between letters when you are sharing books with her, especially the letters that occur in her name and the names of other family members. Once she has reached this stage, you can help a lot by talking about letters when you are writing things down. You might, for example, say, 'I want to write the word "dog", now what letters do I need for d/o/g/?' Also, when you are out and about, point out the various signs that you see – for example, STOP – saying something like 'You know what this says, don't you? STOP. See, it's s/t/o/p/.'

The important thing is to keep the activity light and fun. This sort of development takes time, but you really can help by engaging in some of the simple games given above.

S.T.O.P.

Frequently asked questions

Q : **I feel very confused because not everyone seems to agree about phonics. You talk to some people who say it's extremely important, while others disagree. I don't know what to believe. Can you help?**

A : The great phonics debate has been running for many years and will probably continue to do so, so let's just use a bit of common sense. English is not a totally phonetic language, and while 'sounding out' the letters of a word will help a child to read some words (roughly a third of the English language is phonetic) it won't help him to read words such as 'enough' and 'meringue'. Words such as these must be learned as a whole word, and the most useful thing you can do to assist your child is to explain this to him. If he can't work out a word by sounding it out, he will then know to use another method: for example, making an informed guess at the word based on what he can read. Phonics is only one of the tools a child uses when making sense of print, and its use should not be a case of 'either/or'. When learning to read, children need a range of support structures, especially when they are dealing with a language as complex as English.

Q : **I have heard a lot on the news about something called synthetic phonics. They say it's useful in helping children learn to read, but I don't really understand what it is. Can you explain?**

A : Synthetic phonics teaches children the 'building block' sounds made by letters or groups of letters which, when put together, make words. It differs from analytic phonics, which teaches children larger chunks within words – particularly rhyming words such as 'thought', 'bought', 'sought'. Academics have argued for decades about the role of phonics in teaching reading. The primary national strategy says phonics are essential but not sufficient, and we would agree with this view.

Synthetic phonics is a highly structured approach, which can be successful in helping children to read words but will not necessarily turn them into enthusiastic, well-rounded readers. To do this, a much broader approach is needed – one that enables children to learn phonics through play and games and through sharing quality books and stories with adults. The amount you learn is commensurate with the amount of fun you are having, and this is especially true for young children.

chapter seven

Moving into writing

Writing is the most difficult of the three Rs, because when you write you have so many things to think about at the same time. However, if you have carried out some of the activities on the previous pages, you can be certain that you have done a great deal to prepare your child for the various aspects of writing. Writing needs:

- confidence and competence in speaking and listening, a good vocabulary and a well-developed auditory memory (chapters 1, 2 and 3);

- familiarity with the patterns of written language through hearing and repeating favourite stories (chapter 4);

- knowledge of the alphabet names and letter shapes (chapter 5);

- an understanding of what writing is and what it is for (chapter 5);

- an understanding of how phonic knowledge is involved in converting spoken words into written letters (chapter 6);

- the ability to hear the sounds of the English language and understand the ways in which speech sounds are represented in writing (chapter 6).

Writing also requires a lot of physical control. Manoeuvring a pencil across a page can be a very daunting task for a young child, and if you ask her to do this before she is physically ready you run the risk of creating real, long-term problems. No one likes to do things that are impossibly difficult, and if your child is put in a position where this happens too frequently she will become frustrated and demotivated.

In short, by starting too soon you can actually turn a child off writing, and once she has been turned off it is very difficult to reverse this situation. So, do make sure that your child is not asked to do too much too early. If you wait until she is keen and interested she will learn much more easily. It's fine to let her write and make marks as part of her play. Also, it's really important that she learns about letters and how to form them. However, she has to be ready for the small-scale, careful writing of letters if she is to remain enthusiastic about writing. If you find that she is not enjoying the process of writing, carry on with the activities in the previous chapters.

When deciding whether a child is ready to write letters and words, you may find it useful to examine her drawings. As a rule of thumb, if she is still drawing people with the arms and legs coming out of the head (like those shown here on the left), she is not yet ready to cope with the complex patterns in letters and words. At this stage, help her to notice more features and put more detail in her drawings. As soon as she is drawing a person with a head, body, legs and arms (like the drawing on the right), you can start introducing writing.

Preparing your child for handwriting

Before your child can cope with the fine muscle movements required for handwriting he must develop his large muscles, so make sure that he has plenty of opportunities for developing this control through activities that involve balancing and climbing. Also ensure that he is able to develop his manipulative skills by using tools such as cooking utensils and scissors, and support him to develop hand-eye co-ordination by playing with toys such as jigsaws and Lego®.

Working big

You will need: chubby markers and really large pieces of paper. (Old rolls of wallpaper are very good for this purpose.)
Writing begins with large-scale movements from the shoulder, so encourage your child to practise the action. Have fun creating patterns side by side.

Decorator's brushes

You will need: a set of cheap decorator's brushes.
Let your child 'paint' with water on the outside walls of the house. This will really get her working from the shoulder.

Old squeezy bottles

You will need: old squeezy bottles filled with water.
Allow your child to play with the bottles in the garden. This will help him to develop co-ordination and control.

Writing with salt

You will need: a container of salt and a tray.
Let your child pour the salt out on to the tray. If the container is too heavy, show your child how to fill a salt cellar and pour the salt to make patterns on the tray. Once he has poured all the salt, he can refill the salt cellar and start again. Encourage him to try creating shapes, pictures and letters.

Sweeping up

You will need: a sweeping brush.
Using a sweeping brush will assist development of the large muscles. If your child finds it hard to manipulate the brush, cut the handle down to make a child-sized brush.

Write in sand

You will need: sand (or flour).
If you have a sandpit in the garden or the park, or when you visit the seaside, make marks in the sand. If this is not possible, sieve some flour on to a tray and encourage your child to form shapes in the flour.

Playground chalk

You will need: some chubby sticks of chalk (many of the 'budget' stationers now sell these) and a flat area of concrete. For cleaning up afterwards you will need: a bucket of soapy water and a broom (alternatively, you could use a hosepipe).

Show your child a suitable place outside where he can draw on the concrete, and at the same time explain clearly that drawing should be done only in specially designated places. Demonstrate how to use the chalk on the concrete to make large pictures and letters. Once he has tired of this activity, ask him to help you wash the concrete clean by scrubbing it with the broom and soapy water. Doing this will further develop the movements for handwriting.

If you are unhappy about your child drawing on the concrete, why not attach a large piece of hardboard to a shed or garage. This can then be painted with blackboard paint and used for the same purpose.

Patterns in shaving foam or hair gel

You will need: some shaving foam or hair gel and a large plastic tray or other suitable surface.

Cover the surface of the tray with foam or gel and let your child use his fingers to make patterns and letters in it. If he uses the space up fairly quickly, you may be able to smooth it over and let him have another go before the foam collapses.

You should remain with your child throughout this activity to ensure that he does not put the foam or gel in his mouth.

Fun with icing

You will need: some icing sugar, food colouring, a cake decorator's icing bag and some greaseproof paper or foil.

Mix the icing sugar with a little food colouring and some water, to make a moderately firm paste. Spoon the paste into the icing bag. Then let your child make patterns, pictures or letters on the greaseproof paper or foil, by squeezing the icing out of the bag.

Things you can buy

Your child may also enjoy using various manufactured products to support his writing development. Perhaps the most popular of these are magic drawing boards and magnetic drawing boards. They usually come with a stylus which can be used for mark-making, but initially at least you may prefer to leave such implements aside until your child's finger muscles are more fully developed. Generations of children have been captivated as their drawing or writing vanishes in front of their eyes as they peel back the surface on a magic drawing board or shake the iron filings within the magnetic drawing board. A newer version of this type of drawing toy is Aquadraw®, which comes with a water-based pen. As your child's patterns dry, they also disappear as if by magic.

Letter formation

You will probably find that your child will want to write her name long before the teaching of writing begins in earnest. If so, consult the staff at her nursery or school to find out how they tackle letter formation, and how best you can help. Most schools provide guidance for parents, and some will give you a card with your child's name, demonstrating the correct formation. It is really worthwhile taking the time to do this, as it will ensure that your child does not receive conflicting information.

To teach your child to write her name, begin with skywriting (writing in the air) with her hand and forearm, then follow this by using a marker pen on a large piece of paper. (Marker pens are better than pencils in the early stages of writing as making a mark with a pencil requires much more strength and pressure.)

Holding a pencil puts strain on the thumb and the first two fingers of the writing hand. If children are asked to write at any length before these muscles are strong enough, the act of writing can be physically painful. When writing becomes associated with pain, it is not going to be something that your child enjoys, and she could easily be put off. Make sure therefore that you don't ask her to do too much. Instead, help to develop her finger muscles by engaging in some of the following enjoyable activities.

Once she is keen and interested in writing for herself, there are lots of other ways in which you can assist: for example, by showing her the correct way to hold the pencil. If she finds it difficult to adjust her grip, place the pencil appropriately between her fingers and lightly guide her hand as she writes.

Creative activities

Let your child have fun, for example, by:

- playing with dough and plasticine

- making things with scissors, staplers, hole punches, treasury tags and boxes

- sprinkling glitter and sand

- painting with fingers and different-sized paintbrushes.

Building and making

Help your child, for example, to:

- use tools such as screwdrivers, hammers and pliers (under supervision)

- play with construction equipment such as Stickle Bricks® and Lego®

- weave, sew and thread

- use cooking utensils, garlic presses, pastry cutters and icing bags.

Sorting and sequencing

Your child may like to spend many happy hours, for example:

- picking up buttons, beads, sequins or pasta, and arranging them with fingers and tweezers

- sorting out items of washing and pegging them on to a washing line.

Play equipment

Encourage your child to play with, for example:

- collections of nuts and bolts, locks and keys

- finger puppets

- jigsaws.

Finger rhymes involving finger play

Rhymes such as the following can be recited alone or in groups:

Here's the church and here's the steeple,

Open the door and here are the people.

First they sing and then they pray,

And then they quietly walk away.

For the third line: hold the hands still
and for the fourth line: wiggle fingers and move hands apart.

Daily routines

There are many day-to-day tasks that your child will gain pleasure from doing, for example:

- helping to prepare fruit and vegetables

- putting on and buttoning or zipping coats and other clothes

- tying bows on shoelaces

- helping out with the gardening: for example, planting seeds and pulling out weeds

- sticking stamps on to envelopes

- sorting and counting out money from your purse

- attaching pieces of paper together with paperclips.

Lists, lists, lists

Whenever shopping is required, ask your child to help you compose the list. Involve her in 'to do' lists, Christmas card lists and 'things to take on holiday' lists.

Letters, postcards and emails

Let your child 'help' when you are sending communications to friends and family members. Even though she may do only a small amount, she will learn much from being involved.

Cards and invitations

Most children's first experiences with writing are through Christmas and birthday cards, and party invitations, so do involve your child in this type of writing. Show her how to write 'love' and her name. Encourage her to have a go by herself if she wants to.

Provide a special place for writing

Children love to have their own desk, even if it's just a table in the corner of the room, so provide a special place where they can write with a range of materials. If at all possible, include:

- paper in assorted colours
- stationery and envelopes
- pens, pencils, felt-tip pens and wax crayons
- child safety scissors, stapler and hole punch
- glue stick and adhesive tape
- clipboard
- alphabet book
- ruler, rubber and pencil sharpener
- elastic bands
- picture dictionary.

Left-handed children

It is generally believed that there are now more left-handed children than ever before. The reality, however, is that there are no more left-handers than previously; it is just that, thankfully, left-handed children are no longer forced to write with their right hands. Many adults can relate horror stories of having their left hands held behind their backs as they struggled to write letters in a way that for them was completely unnatural. In many cases, this caused long-term psychological damage.

Many children take quite a while to work out which is their preferred hand, and some are naturally ambidextrous. Therefore, watch your child carefully to see which hand appears to be the dominant one. For example, when you hand her something, which hand does she use as she reaches for the object? If she picks something up from the floor, which hand does she use? You may notice a definite preference. However, if your child seems happy to work with either hand, try gently to guide her towards the right. She lives in a right-hand orientated world, and life as a right-hander is actually easier.

Once you are certain that your child is left-handed, you can help her by providing a pair of left-handed scissors so she isn't disadvantaged when she is cutting (see the resources list on pages 94–95). When your child is ready to start doing basic handwriting movements, letter formation and, eventually, handwriting itself, she will need special attention. As a left-hander, it is especially important that she learns the correct posture and pen grip as well as how to form and join letters properly. If you (or a friend or carer) is left-handed, you can show your child what to do. If not, you need to train yourself to demonstrate how to form letters using your left hand.

It is also helpful to show your child how to slant her paper so that her hand as she writes is not covering what she has just written. The best position is for the bottom of the page to be angled to the left, at about 30 degrees to the vertical. If a left-handed child doesn't learn how to position the paper correctly, she could end up trying to arch her wrist in order to see what she has just written, and when she is older and asked to write at length this can lead to cramp. At school, check out that your child is seated with space on her left-hand side so that she does not collide with a right-hander, whose writing arm would naturally be moving close to her. Also, buy her useful equipment such as a left-handed ruler and pencil sharpener.

Frequently asked questions

Q : **My daughter was showing an interest in writing when she was three and a half. My son is now five and a half and still has little inclination to write. He would much rather be outside tearing about. Why is this and what can I do about it?**

A : This is not at all uncommon. It is now widely accepted that there are distinct differences in the way that boys and girls acquire language and literacy skills. The brains of males and females are subtly different, and the part of the brain that processes language is actually larger in females than in males. By contrast, males tend to demonstrate better abilities in spatial tasks. It is as if the anatomy of the brain is more supportive to girls, making language acquisition easier. And then, of course, there is testosterone. At around the same time as boys begin formal schooling, they receive a huge surge of testosterone, causing a growth spurt and energetic and vigorous behaviour. They seem to have boundless energy, and their play is full of action and adventure.

Although boys catch up eventually, they can be damaged if they are 'forced' into writing too soon. So do try to be patient. As long as you engage in some of the activities in this chapter and try not to pressurize too much, your son will get there in the end. It is very understandable that this lack of interest is causing you concern, but feel reassured that a huge number of boys who have worried their parents silly then learned to write in the space of a few months once the brain was ready. It is important to remember that there are exceptions to every rule; some boys will start to write earlier than their peers, and some girls do so later than boys.

NB Very few children experience profound difficulties with writing. If your child falls into this category, his school will be sure to alert you to these problems, and specialist help can be sought.

Q : **My child has started to write, but his letters are enormous. Should I worry about this?**

A : Not at all, this is quite normal. Writing requires a wide range of skills, one of which is control of the finger muscles. For many young children, this technique takes time to develop. Keep an eye on his writing and over time you will notice a real difference. With practice, his writing will show increased control and gradually become smaller. You should just keep on doing all of the activities suggested in this chapter for increasing the strength of his finger muscles.

Frequently asked questions *continued*

Q : My child is left-handed. Does this mean that he will find writing more difficult, and is there anything I can do to assist him?

A : Approximately 12 per cent of the population are left-handed, and boys are more likely to be left-handed than girls. When it comes to handwriting, things will be far easier if you have a left-handed adult in the family. Such a person will be able to show the child how to form his letters. If you are not that fortunate, train yourself to teach the movements left-handed. (This is easier than you may think.) It will also help if you buy some left-handed scissors (see the resources list on pages 94–95).

Q : How can I tell if my child is ready for writing?

A : In the first instance you will notice that he becomes fascinated by writing and using pens, pencils and other writing materials. When this occurs, look carefully at his drawings. Children draw before they write, and their drawings tell you much about their readiness for writing. As a general rule, children should be able to draw a picture of a person with a head, body, arms and legs in the correct positions. If your child is still drawing with the arms and legs coming out of the head, he needs much more experience of drawing before he progresses on to writing.

Q : I know that my child should form his letters properly, but I am not sure what 'properly' is. How can I find out?

A : The first thing that young children usually want to write is their name. Frequently, they want to do this long before they are really ready for formal instruction in handwriting. If your child fits this description, do teach him how to form the letters correctly, if necessary, by gently guiding his hand. (If he falls into the habit of forming letters incorrectly, it can be difficult to reverse this.) His school will want you to teach the letters using a capital for the first letter of the name and the rest of the letters in lower case. If you are in any doubt about this, ask your child's teacher – most schools produce guidance for parents on correct letter formation. Alternatively, you can look at the handwriting groups and jingles on pages 90–93.

Frequently asked questions *continued*

Q : **My child doesn't seem to be able to decide whether he is left-handed or right-handed. He uses both hands when writing. What can I do about this?**

A : For some children, deciding which hand is their dominant one can take quite some time. In fact, it is not unusual for some children still to be undecided when they start school. If your child seems happy to use either hand, it is a good idea to guide him gently into using the right hand. However, no child should ever be forced into using his right hand, because this can cause real, long-term damage. A child who is naturally left-handed should always be supported to use his left hand. Some children, however, are truly ambidextrous.

Q : **My child seems to have difficulty holding a pencil. Although I have shown him how to do it properly, he still insists on gripping it the wrong way. What can I do?**

A : Without putting too much pressure on your child, gently remind him of the correct pencil grip and keep an eye on things. Most importantly, try to ensure that when he is writing he keeps his wrist on the writing surface. Unless he does this, he will be prone to getting cramp in his hand when he is older and required to write at greater length. Do everything you can to encourage the correct grip but not to the extent where he becomes distressed. What matters most is that his writing is legible. Many adults hold their pencil in an unconventional way but still manage to produce legible writing.

Q : **My three-year-old child makes lots of scribbles that he calls writing. When he showed his 'writing' to his grandmother she told him that it was just a load of scribble. Is this the right thing to do?**

A : Not at all. Your child's scribbles are his 'writing,' and as time goes on they will begin to look more and more like conventional writing. The important thing is to maintain your child's interest, so do praise and admire his scribbles and carry out the activities suggested in this chapter. He will be able to form more recognizable letters as he matures!

Appendix

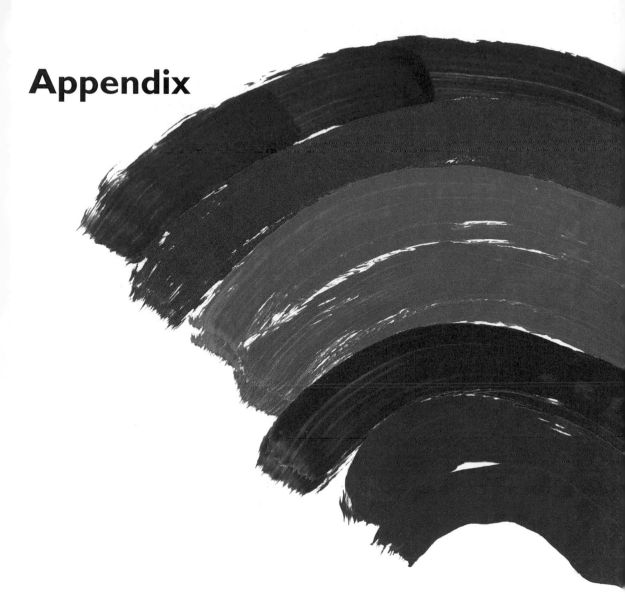

Handwriting groups and jingles

The ∫ group

l	t

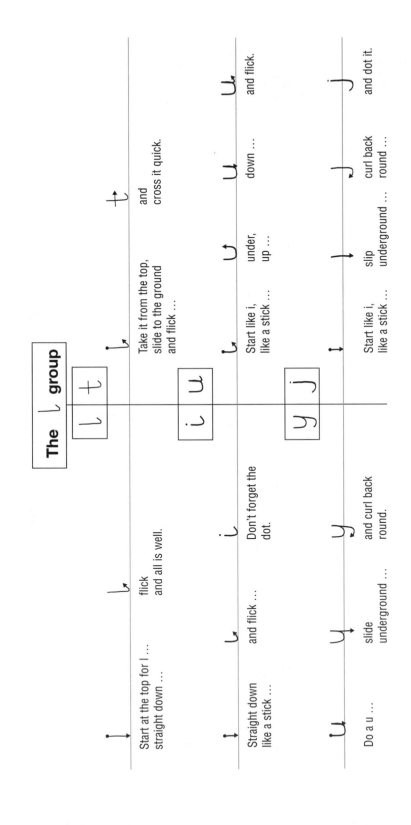

Start at the top for l …
straight down …

flick
and all is well.

Take it from the top,
slide to the ground
and flick …

and
cross it quick.

i	u

Straight down
like a stick …

and flick …

Don't forget the
dot.

Start like i,
like a stick …

under,
up …

down …

and flick.

y	j

Do a u …

slide
underground …

and curl back
round.

Start like i,
like a stick …

slip
underground …

curl back
round …

and dot it.

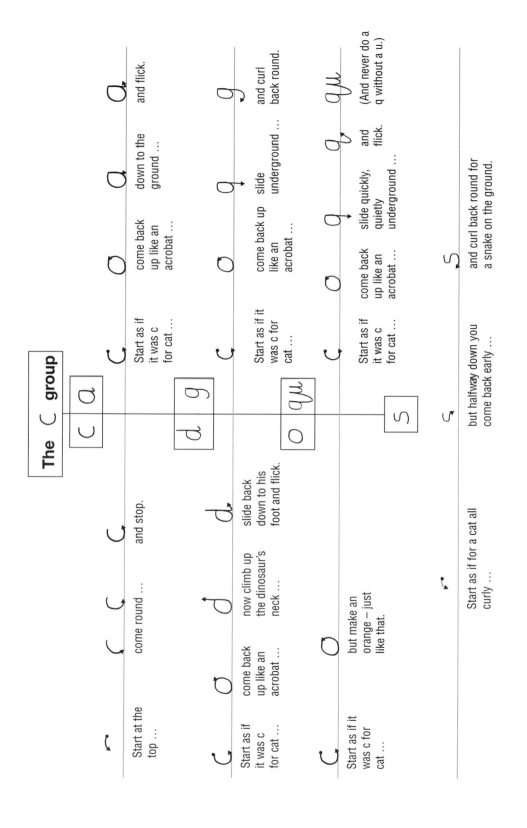

The c group

c — Start at the top … come round … and stop.

a — Start as if it was c for cat … come back up like an acrobat … down to the ground … and flick.

d — Start as if it was c for cat … come back up like an acrobat … now climb up the dinosaur's neck … slide back down to his foot and flick.

g — Start as if it was c for cat … come back up like an acrobat … slide underground … and curl back round.

o — Start as if it was c for cat … come back up like an acrobat … but make an orange – just like that.

qu — Start as if it was c for cat … come back up like an acrobat … slide quickly, quietly underground … and flick. (And never do a q without a u.)

s — Start as if for a cat all curly … but halfway down you come back early … and curl back round for a snake on the ground.

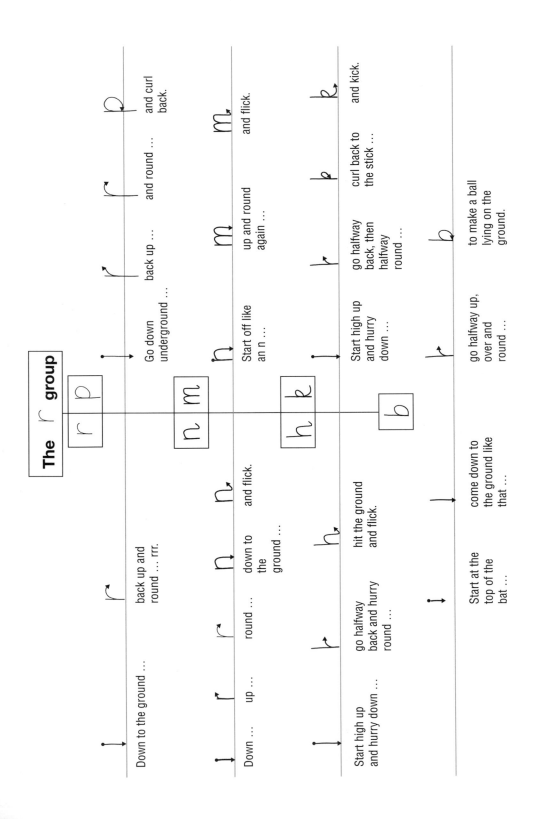

The r group

r p

Down to the ground ... back up and round ... rrr.

Go down underground ... back up ... and round ... and curl back.

n m

Down ... up ... round ... down to the ground ... and flick.

Start off like an n ... up and round again ... and flick.

h k

Start high up and hurry down ... go halfway back and hurry round ... hit the ground and flick.

Start high up and hurry down ... go halfway back, then halfway round ... curl back to the stick ... and kick.

b

Start at the top of the bat ... come down to the ground like that ... go halfway up, over and round ... to make a ball lying on the ground.

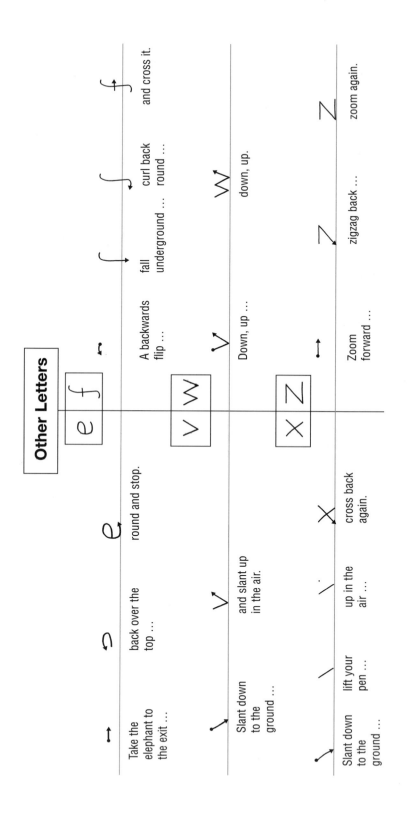

Other Letters

e
Take the elephant to the exit … back over the top … round and stop.

f
A backwards flip … fall underground … curl back round … and cross it.

v
Slant down to the ground … and slant up in the air.

w
Down, up … down, up.

x
Slant down to the ground … lift your pen … up in the air … cross back again.

z
Zoom forward … zigzag back … zoom again.

Recommended resources

Chapter I: Learning to listen

Faber, Adele and Mazlish, Elaine (2001), *How to talk so kids will listen and listen so kids will talk*, Piccadilly, London

Robb, Jean and Letts, Hilary (1997), *Creating kids who can concentrate*, Hodder & Stoughton, London

Chapter 2: Time to talk

Bayley, Ros and Broadbent, Lynn (2004), *Talking cards: talking with Twinkle*, Lawrence Educational Publications, Walsall (tel: 01922 643833; www.educationalpublications.com)

Bayley, Ros and Broadbent, Lynn (2003), *The foundation stage at home*, Lawrence Educational Publications, Walsall (tel: 01922 643833; www.educationalpublications.com)

Chapter 3: Music, movement and memory

Bayley, Ros and Broadbent, Lynn (2003), *Helping young children with steady beat* and *The rap pack* (Pack comprises four little books of raps and two CDs), Lawrence Educational Publications, Walsall (tel: 01922 643833; www.educationalpublications.com)

Caroe, Linda (1999), *Carousel* (CD), songs for developing language skills, Carousel Music Workshop, Eastbourne (tel: 01323 734418)

Scott, Steve and Bone, Greg (2005), *Keeping the beat* (CD of traditional songs played in an upbeat modern style), Keeping the Beat Productions, Bromley, Kent (tel: 020 8402 9355; www.keepingthebeat.co.uk)

Chapter 4: Storytime

For an excellent range of puppets: Puppets by Post (tel: 01462 446040; www.puppetsbypost.com)

Chapter 5: Learning about print

Bromley, Helen (2004), *Helping young children to learn to read*, Lawrence Educational Publications, Walsall (tel: 01922 643833; www.educationalpublications.com)

Chapter 6: Tuning into sound: (see recommendations on page 69)

Chapter 7: Moving into writing

McEwan, Suzanne and McEwan, Lucy (2003), *This is the way I learnt to write*, Lawrence Educational Publications, Walsall (tel: 01922 643833; www.educationalpublications.com)

For left-handed children, equipment (such as scissors, pencil sharpeners and rulers) and a video demonstrating practice and advice on pencil grip and how to teach handwriting are available from Anything Left-handed, 5 Charles Street, Worcester WR1 2AQ (tel: 01905 25798; www.lefthand-education.co.uk)

For books that support all the above areas:

Biddulph, Steve (2003), *Raising boys*, Thorsons, London

Hannaford, Carla (1995), *Smart moves, why learning is not all in your head*, Great Ocean, Arlington, Va

Lucas, Bill and Smith, Alistair (2002), *Help your child to succeed*, Network Educational Press, Stafford

Palmer, Sue (Spring 2006), *Toxic childhood: How contemporary culture is damaging the next generation ... and what we can do about it*, Orion Books, London

Useful websites

www.dfes.gov.uk	Information on the Foundation Stage curriculum. Also follow link to the parents' centre aspect of the website
www.home-start.org.uk	Also links to other potentially useful websites
www.parentcentre.gov.uk	Information on the Foundation Stage curriculum
www.surestart.gov.uk	Information on government programmes to deliver early education, health, childcare and family support
www.skillsforfamilies.org	Ideas, activities and guidance for literacy and numeracy
www.underfives.co.uk	Information for parents, free resources
www.booktrust.org.uk	Supports reading with very young children
www.bgfl.org	Has a range of games and activities for young children
www.bbc.co.uk/cbeebies	Information, games and activities
www.crayola.com	Resources and ideas
www.funwithspot.com	Spot the Dog's official website; includes resources and activities
www.ladybird.co.uk	Games, activities and books online

Publisher's acknowledgements

Acknowledgements and thanks are due to the following for permission to use copyright material:
Lynda Lawrence for the verses from *The rap pack* (Lawrence Educational Publications 2003);
Lucy McEwan and Lawrence Educational Publishers for the first child's artwork on page 76;
Sue Palmer and Ros Bayley for the handwriting groups and jingles from *Foundations of Literacy* (Network Educational Press 2004).

A selection of titles from Network Educational Press

Help Your Child to Succeed: The essential guide for parents by Bill Lucas and Alistair Smith

Foundations of Literacy: A balanced approach to language, listening and literacy skills in the early years by Sue Palmer and Ros Bayley

Parents' and Carers' Guide for Able and Talented Children by Barry Teare

The Thinking Child: Brain-based learning for the foundation stage by Nicola Call with Sally Featherstone

The Thinking Child Resource Book by Nicola Call with Sally Featherstone

Becoming Emotionally Intelligent by Catherine Corrie

Promoting Children's Well-Being in the Primary Years edited by Andrew Burrell and Jeni Riley

Practical Guide to Revision Techniques by Simon Percival

Discover Your Hidden Talents: The essential guide to lifelong learning by Bill Lucas

Future Directions: Practical ways to develop emotional intelligence and confidence in young people by Diane Carrington and Helen Whitten

But Why? Developing philosophical thinking in the classroom by Sara Stanley with Steve Bowkett

This pack includes four delightfully illustrated picture books also available separately:

Philosophy Bear and the Big Sky by Steve Bowkett

If I Were a Spider by Steve Bowkett

Pinocchio: The Cricket's Tale retold by Sara Stanley

Dojen the Wanderer by Steve Bowkett

This is Science! Learning science through songs and stories (Key Stage 1) by Tim Harding

That's Science! Learning science through songs (Key Stage 2) by Tim Harding

That's Maths! Learning maths through songs (Key Stage 2) by Tim Harding

That's English! Learning English through songs (Key Stage 2) by Tim Harding

For sample book pages, more information and ordering details, please visit our website www.networkpress.co.uk